OLD NORSE MYTHOLOGY

T0244334

World Mythology in Theory and Everyday Life

Series Editors: Tok Thompson and Gregory Schrempp

This series presents an innovative and accessible overview of the world's mythological traditions. The inaugural volume provides a theoretical introduction to the study of myth, while the individual case studies from throughout time and around the world help guide the reader through the wondrous complexity and diversity of myths, and their widespread influences in human cultures, societies, and everyday lives.

The Truth of Myth: World Mythology in Theory and Everyday Life
Tok Thompson and Gregory Schrempp

Old Norse Mythology
John Lindow

OLD NORSE MYTHOLOGY

John Lindow

OXFORD

UNIVERSITY PRESS

OXFORD
UNIVERSITY PRESS

Oxford University Press is a department of the University of Oxford. It furthers
the University's objective of excellence in research, scholarship, and education
by publishing worldwide. Oxford is a registered trade mark of Oxford University
Press in the UK and certain other countries.

Published in the United States of America by Oxford University Press
198 Madison Avenue, New York, NY 10016, United States of America.

Library of Congress Cataloging-in-Publication Data
Names: Lindow, John, author.
Title: Old Norse mythology / John Lindow.
Description: New York : Oxford University Press, 2021. |
Includes bibliographical references and index.
Identifiers: LCCN 2020024611 (print) | LCCN 2020024612 (ebook) |
ISBN 9780190852252 (hardback) | ISBN 9780197554487 (paperback) |
ISBN 9780190852276 (epub)
Subjects: LCSH: Mythology, Norse. | Old Norse literature—History and criticism. |
Icelandic literature—History and criticism.
Classification: LCC BL860 .L58 2020 (print) | LCC BL860 (ebook) |
DDC 293/.13—dc23
LC record available at https://lccn.loc.gov/2020024611
LC ebook record available at https://lccn.loc.gov/2020024612

CONTENTS

PREFACE

This book treats from the perspective of the series World Mythology in Theory and Everyday Life the body of texts from medieval Scandinavia, mostly Iceland, usually known as "Norse mythology" or "Scandinavian mythology." Specifically, it constitutes a case study of a "literary or textual mythology," that is, a mythology from the past that we know only through written texts that have been left to us, augmented in a few cases by artifacts and images. This case is particularly interesting because the texts (with a tiny handful of enigmatic exceptions) were recorded centuries after the Nordic peoples had abandoned the religion associated with the mythology and converted to Christianity. The mythology lived on without direct connection to ritual activity or religious conviction.

Drawing both on sources from before the conversion and on comparative analysis, it is certainly possible to reach informed inferences about the mythology before the conversion to Christianity—that is, when it existed as part of the pre-Christian religion of the Nordic peoples and their successors. From the perspective of the mythologies of the world, what is perhaps most important about these inferences is that this pre-Christian mythology was not a canonical mythology, since it almost certainly lacked a canon of sacred texts such as one finds in the great world religions of today. It is far more analogous to Greek mythology, where we find numerous versions of the same story, from different times and places, often contradicting one other in ways great and small.

The focus of the book is not the mythology in and of itself, as would be true of a handbook (for information on handbooks and other such works, see "Suggestions for Further Readings" following the Conclusion), but rather how particular historical and intellectual circumstances formed conceptions about it. Thus the summary of the mythology itself (chapter 1), although it does try to mention the important myths and recognizes variation and contradiction, presents it as a more coherent narrative, more or less a system, rather than as an assortment of gods and stories. Chapter 2 takes a look at texts and artifacts that reflect one myth as sacred narrative, namely Þórr fishing up the World Serpent, a monster that encircles the earth in the offshore waters. Although we do have both texts and images from the pre-Christian period describing this central myth, the texts are difficult, and interpretation of the images depends on the texts. My analysis is quite detailed in places, but I believe that the reader who pays attention will be rewarded with a fresh view of how the texts work and of the stability and variation of the motifs involved. The chapter also takes on the challenges presented in the texts that are obviously from the Christian period. Chapter 3 explores the how and why of the survival of the myths in Christian medieval Scandinavia, primarily through the medieval theory know as euhemerism, according to which the gods in the mythology reflected real humans who had lived in the past. Writing about them was thus to some degree to write history and distanced authors like Saxo Grammaticus, historian of the Danish realm, or Snorri Sturluson, author of *Edda*, a handbook of poetics, from the pagan past. The chapter shows in some detail how Snorri's *Edda* relied heavily on this theory. Snorri's motive with the work, however, was to save from oblivion the language of poetry, and thus the poetry itself. This aspect of the study of Old Norse mythology has up to now more or less been specialist rather than general knowledge. Chapter 4 treats the relationship of Old Norse mythology to various ideologies. Some of these probably go back to the pre-Christian period, such as ideologies surrounding kingship. Others have to do with the creation of suitably impressive pasts for the then powerful nation-states of Denmark and Sweden in the seventeenth and early eighteenth centuries, with the notions of national romanticism in the late eighteenth and nineteenth centuries, and with the search for Germanic purity that has tainted political and religious movements. The chapter ends by showing the ideologies at work in both literary and popular culture in the twentieth and twenty-first centuries. In the Conclusion I draw together the previous chapters to consider the question of the relationship between Old Norse mythology and the notion of myth as sacred narrative.

Translations of the *Poetic Edda* are from Carolyne Larrington, *The Poetic Edda*;[1] of Snorri Sturluson's *Edda* from Anthony Faulkes, *Snorri Sturluson: Edda*; and of the *Gesta Danorum* of Saxo Grammaticus from the translation by Peter Fisher in the edition by Karsten Friis-Jensen. All are accurate and informed by deep learning. In citing the work of these and other translators I retain the punctuation, spelling, and name forms they use, although in my text I use the Old Norse forms of the name. Thus in these translations one may see, for example, *Geirrod*, where I will write *Geirrøðr*, or *Hod*, where I will write *Hǫðr*. Occasionally I comment on alternate possibilities for the translations, or alternate manuscript readings, but only when it is necessary for a clearer understanding of the mythology. Translations from skaldic poetry (which I will call *dróttkvætt* poetry—see the Introduction) are from the admirable new edition of that corpus by a coalition of scholars. In that edition, poetic synonyms (*heiti*) are glossed <thus> and kennings explicated [THUS]; kennings are explained in the Introduction.

Guide to Pronunciation

Because most scholars today, although not all, use modern Icelandic pronunciation, the following guide aims for that pronunciation.

a   like *a* in *father*
á   like *ou* in f*ou*nd
e   like *e* in b*e*t
é   like *ye* in *ye*llow
i   like *i* in *i*diot
í   like e in med*i*a
o   like *aw* in *aw*ful
ó   like *ow* in l*ow*
u   like German *ü*, or Valley Girl *eww*
ú   like *oo* in w*oo*
æ   like *i* in f*i*le
œ   like *i* in f*i*le
ø   like *oo* in b*oo*k
ǫ   like *oo* in b*oo*k
au like *oi* in b*oi*l
ey like *ay* in pl*ay*
ð   like th in fa*th*er
þ   like *th* in *th*orn

Notes

1. Because I retain the Old Norse titles and Larrington translates them, I give her translation of a given poem's title at its first mention in the pages below. The poems are also to be found in the Index, under the Old Norse titles with Larrington's translated titles appended; this I hope will offer the reader an easy way to move between the two title forms.

ACKNOWLEDGMENTS

I am grateful to Anders Andrén and Cecilia Ljung for allowing me to profit from the work they have done identifying images related to Nordic pre-Christian religion, including their own photographs. I gained preliminary information about many of the images from the captions Andrén wrote for those that are used in the volumes of *Pre-Christian Religions of the North: History and Structures*, edited by Andrén, Jens Peter Schjødt, and myself (Schjødt et al. 2020). Also enormous thanks to Henning Kure for helping me obtain images from the Danish *Valhalla* series.

Introduction

From Oral to Written Mythology

The title of this book, *Old Norse Mythology*, recognizes the fact that the mythology in question is recorded almost exclusively in the manuscripts of Old Norse literary tradition—that is, in manuscripts primarily from thirteenth- and fourteenth-century Iceland (the term "Old Norse" recognizes that the language in question was spoken in Norway, Iceland, and other Atlantic islands). Since Iceland had converted to Christianity in the year 1000 CE, the scribes who recorded the myths were Christians, and the myths can hardly have been sacred in their eyes. Nevertheless, there were mythographers such as Snorri Sturluson (1179–1241), who composed *Edda* (c. 1220–1230), a handbook of poetics that includes much information about the mythology, including synopses of many myths, and such as the anonymous redactor of what we now call the *Poetic Edda* (c. 1250?), a collection of mythic and heroic poems; and myths are displaced into history in the *Gesta Danorum* "History of the Danes" by Saxo Grammaticus, c. 1200. This chapter discusses the progression from the oral mythology of the Viking Age (c. 800–1100) and before to the written mythology of the Middle Ages.

The Viking Age, c. 800–1100, is part of the Scandinavian Late Iron Age, c. 550–1100; the Iron Age in Scandinavia began c. 200 BCE.

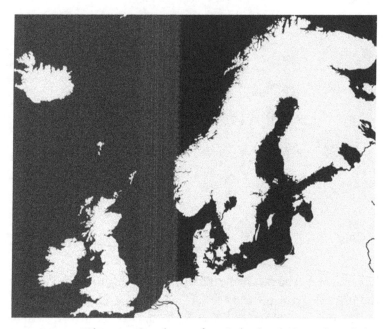

FIGURE I.1 Viking Age Scandinavia, from Iceland to the West through the British Isles to the South to Finland and Russia to the East. Map: Based on Europe and North America Map, Wikimedia Commons.

See figure I.1 for a map of Viking Age Scandinavia, which was more extensive than the Scandinavian peninsula and the Danish territory that we think of today as comprising Scandinavia. Figure I.2 shows the districts of mainland Scandinavia and demonstrates that older settlement was along the coasts and in the fertile inland areas.

During the period c. 600–800 CE, Scandinavian languages diverged linguistically from related languages of the Germanic family, which included Gothic, Old English, Old High German, and Old Saxon. These in turn were part of the Indo-European family of languages, and it is quite likely that some religious and mythological structures were "inherited" from the Indo-European past, or from the Germanic past, but we must understand such inheritance as dynamic and fluid rather than static.

FIGURE I.2 The districts of Scandinavia. Map: Disir Productions, based on draft by Anders Andrén. Also published in Schjødt et al. 2020.

Even without written sources, we would know something about religion and mythology during and before the Late Iron Age. For example, when the Germanic peoples confronted the Roman weekday names, they translated them. Latin *dies Solis* (day of the Sun) underlies our Sunday, *dies Lunae* (day of the moon) our Monday, *dies Martis* (day of Mars) our Tuesday, *dies Mercurii* (day of Mercury) our Wednesday, *dies Jovis* (day of Jupiter) our Thursday, *dies Veneris* (day of Venus) our Friday, and *dies Saturnis* (day of Saturn) our Saturday. While the Roman weekday names were based on the sun, moon, and planets, these in turn reflected the names of gods, and the Germanic interpretation of the names (usually known in scholarship with the Latin phrase *interpretatio germanica*) will certainly have relied on identifying similarities between native gods and those of the Romans. Sun, Moon, and Saturn remained untranslated (the latter at least in English and some German areas— in other German areas it became "Sunday eve" and in Scandinavia it became "wash-day"). The other names contain "translations" or interpretations: Mars was equated with *Tīwaz (Old English Tīw, Old High German Ziu, Old Norse Týr); Mercury with *Wōþanaz (Old English Wodæn, Old High German Wotan, Old Norse Óðinn [Odin]); Jupiter with *Þun(a)raz (Old English Þonar, Old High German Donar, Old Norse Þórr [Thor]); Venus with *Frijjō (Old English Frīg, Old High German Frī, Old Norse Frigg).[1]

On the basis of these "translations," we can infer that *Tīwaz had some connection with battle, since Mars was a god of war; *Wōþanaz with travel, commerce, theft, and/or trickery, mythological attributes of Mercury; *Þun(a)raz with the sky and lightning, and, like Jupiter, perhaps with pride of place in the pantheon; and *Frijjō with love and possibly fertility. These profiles actually fit

---

[1] Following the convention of historical linguistics, those forms that have been reconstructed from existing forms, but are actually not attested or recorded, are indicated with an initial asterisk. "Sound laws" (the observed development of sound changes) make the reconstructed forms quite trustworthy.

rather nicely with profiles of the relevant gods in Old Norse mythology. Týr is brave and said in some sources to be a god of battle.
Óðinn travels frequently and engages in multiple acts of theft and
trickery; Þórr has a hammer, Mjǫllnir, that may once have been a
thunder-weapon; and Frigg's actions in the mythology stress her
love for her husband Óðinn and son Baldr. As we shall see, the fit is
far from perfect, but it makes clear that many of the notions captured
in the mythology as it was written down by Christian scribes had
long and deep antecedents.

Opposite to the *interpretatio germanica* was what scholars call the
interpretatio romana, the attempt by Roman writers to describe the
religions of the ethnic groups at the fringe of the empire, which they
did for the most part using the names of Roman deities. Toward the
very end of the first century CE, the historian Tacitus wrote a description entitled *Germania* about the territory on the far side of the
Rhine. In ch. 9 he stated:

> Of the gods, they give a special worship to Mercury, to whom on
> certain days they count even the sacrifice of human life lawful.
> Hercules and Mars they appease with such animal life as is permis-
> sible. A section of the Suebi sacrifices also to Isis: the cause and
> origin of this foreign worship I have not succeeded in discovering,
> except that the emblem itself, which takes the shape of a Liburnian
> galley, shows that the ritual is imported. [Petersen 1914: 277]

Using the weekday names, we can infer that Tacitus used Mercury
to refer to *Wōþanaz, and we indeed see human sacrifice to Óðinn
in the much later Scandinavian sources. Mars would again be Týr.
The identity of Hercules we must seek in Roman mythology, where
he is most famous for the Labors imposed upon him by his nemesis Eurystheus; these involve the slaying of some monsters (the
Nemean lion, the nine-head hydra, the Stymphalian birds) and the
neutralizing of others (the Erymanthian boar, the mad bull of Crete,
the man-eating mares of King Diomedes, the three-headed dog

Cerberus), as well as the acquisition of numerous precious objects (the hind of Ceryneia, the girdle of Hypolite, the cattle of Geryon, the golden fleece, the golden apples of the Hesperides). These accord quite closely with the profile of Þórr in the mythology: he kills multiple monsters (one at least with multiple heads), acquires a valuable kettle, and in general makes the world safe (here we might compare not only neutralizing monsters but also mucking out the Augean stables, a concrete analogue to the symbolic "cleansing" of the world that Þórr undertakes through his monster-slaying).

Isis is perhaps more difficult, but if we think again of the weekday names, we would expect a connection with *Frijjō. Although she was originally an Egyptian goddess, Isis was widely worshipped in the Roman empire, and she was, like Frigg in the later Scandinavian sources, famous as wife and mother. Isis was involved with conceptions of death and the afterlife through her partial rescue of her husband Osiris, and Frigg was involved with similar conceptions in her attempts to revive her dead son Baldr. One might also argue that Frigg's attempts to protect Baldr could have paralleled Isis's protection of her son Horus as he grew up. Again, the parallels are enticing but incomplete. For example, it is Freyja, not Frigg, who travels about seeking her lost husband, as does Isis. Furthermore, the ship, a potent symbol in Old Norse mythology, had no connection with Frigg (except perhaps for Baldr's funeral ship) and a far better connection with Freyja's father Njǫrðr and brother Freyr than with Freyja. In addition, Isis was often equated with Ceres, goddess of grain and fertility of the soil, and that characteristic would accord better too with Freyr than with Frigg or even Freyja.

One further point about Tacitus is that he describes a group of three male gods and one female. Writing nearly one thousand years later, the church historian known as Adam of Bremen wrote about a pagan temple in Uppsala,[2] Sweden, where there were idols

[2] The place is now known as Gamla Uppsala (Old Uppsala) and is located a few kilometers from today's Uppsala, which grew up around the new cathedral in the Middle Ages.

of three male gods: Þórr, Óðinn, and not Týr but Freyr (whom he calls Fricco). And the "Old Saxon Baptismal Vow," found in a ninth-century manuscript, calls on Christians to abjure the devil, as well as Thunaer, Uuodan, and Saxnot. Here we recognize German derivatives of *Þun(a)raz and *Wōþanaz. Given the identity of the first syllable of his name with that of the tribe, Saxnot, who also appears in English royal genealogy, must be a name for a chief god of the Saxons and perhaps their progenitor. Although attempts have been made to identify him with Týr, he might just as well have been some other god.

Of course, Hercules was a son of Jupiter who lived his life among humans. Nevertheless, the apparently varying reflections of *Þun(a)raz in the Germanic and Roman "interpretations," or of the existence of the local god's name Saxnot, should not surprise us. There must have been much variation in time and space in the mythology, which was transmitted not in writing but by means of oral tradition. There were thus no written texts to refer to in order to settle questions of variation in mythological ideas, and such variation was surely normal. There were no canonical texts, like a Bible or Quran. Probably ideas were fairly consistent at any given time in any given place in any given social group, but we cannot even prove that. We do know that although there were religious specialists—persons who fulfilled specific religious functions—there was no priestly class per se, that is, probably no persons whose sole duty it was to preside over religious activities such as ritual.

Evidence of the cults of the gods of the *interpretatio germanica* are to be found in theophoric (= referring to a deity) place names in England, Germany, and Scandinavia. Compound names beginning in Týr-, such as Tissø (originally "Týr's lake"), are common in parts of Denmark, with forests and groves the most common second component. Place names beginning in Óðin-/Wodæn- are to be found in Scandinavia and England. Place names beginning in Þór- or the equivalent are to be found across the Germanic area and are widespread in Scandinavia, with particularly dense clustering in the Oslo fjord area and around Lake Mälar in Sweden. Often the Scandinavian Þórr names are connected with so-called central places (places that had extensive trade contacts and legal and cult importance; see figure I.3 for a map of their locations).

Several of the Þórr names in the Oslo fjord area have a second component meaning something like "cult site." Frigg, on the other hand, has left no record in the landscape. Although there must have been extensive variation, the evidence from the *interpretatio germanica* and the theophoric place names makes it clear that at least the three major gods were widely known and worshipped; other place names can be interpreted as theophoric based on evidence from the later mythological sources. Thus we know that the gods of Old Norse mythology were part of the landscape of Iron Age Scandinavia.

Early in *Germania* (ch. 2), Tacitus describes the origin of a basic grouping of the Germanic tribes:

> Their ancient hymns—the only style of record or history which they possess—celebrate a god Tuisto, a scion of the soil, and his son Mannus as the beginning and the founders of their race. To Mannus they ascribe three sons, from whose names the tribes of the sea-shore are to be known as Ingaevones, the central tribes as Herminones, and the rest as Istaevones. [Petersen 1914: 267]

This may be comparted to the myth of the origin of gods and "giants" presented by the Icelander Snorri Sturluson in his *Edda* (c. 1220–1230): a cow named Auðhumla licked a man out of stones in the earth over the course of three days (just as Tuisto was "a scion of the soil"—the Latin literally says that he issued from the earth). This man, whose name was Búri, had a son, named not "man" but "son" (Old Norse Borr or Burr), who in turn had three sons: Óðinn, Vili, and Vé. While there is no indication that these three sons were connected with groupings of tribes, there were royal genealogies that went back to Óðinn.

FIGURE I.3 Map of central places and early towns in southern Scandinavia. Map: Disir productions, Uppsala, based on draft by Anders Andrén. Also published in Schjødt et al. 2020.

These examples will serve to show that we can infer the existence of myths and structures parallel to those that we find in Old Norse mythology over a thousand years before that mythology was recorded by Christian scribes in Iceland, along with the kind of variation we would naturally expect. It must also be stressed, however, that the mythology as we have it also shows "horizontal" influence from other traditions, both within the Indo-European language family, such as Baltic, Slavic, Roman, and outside it, especially Finnish and Sámi.

Tacitus writes that the Germanic tribes preserved the memory of the past, including myths, in the form of "ancient hymns—the only style of record or history which they possess." The translation "hymn" may be a bit misleading; the Latin word, *carmen*, means song or verse, so these would only be hymns if they celebrated deities, and the evidence to be presented just below shows that many other kinds of subject were probably taken up. "Ancient" presumably means that people had been singing these songs, or reciting these poems, for a long time, over generations.

Since we find poetry of more or less the same form recorded in Old Norse, Old English, Old High German, Old Saxon, and in various older and more recent runic inscriptions, it seems probable that the ancient songs to which Tacitus refers had the common features of this later poetry. The formal features include a poetic line with four stressed syllables, two in each half line, the two half-lines linked by alliteration, without a requirement for a set number of syllables in the line. The alliteration always falls on the first stressed syllable of the second half-line (any preceding syllables were unstressed and therefore outside the metrical system). Here are examples from various traditions. The alliterating stressed syllables are indicated by bold type, non-alliterating stressed syllables by italic. Unmarked syllables bore no stress.

Reð **Þjoð**rikR   hinn **þur***mo*ði,
stilliR *flut*na,   **strand**u *Hreið*maraR.

SitiR nu **garu**R   a **gu**ta **sin**um,
skialdi umb *fatl*aðR,   **sk**ati *Mæ*ringa.

Theodoric [once] ruled, the bold one,
ruler of sea-warriors, the shore of the Gothic sea.
He sits now outfitted, on his Gothic horse,
with his shield buckled on, prince of the Mærings.
[Runic inscription on Rök Stone, Östergötland, Sweden, first half
    ninth century]

Hadubrant *gimah*alta,   **Hilt**itbrantes *sun*u:
"dat *sag*etun mi   *us*ere *liut*i,
alte **ant**i frote,   dea **erh**ina *war*un,
dat **Hilt**ibrant hætti min *fat*er: ih **heit**tu **Had**ubrant.

Hadubrant spoke,   the son of Hiltibrant:
Our people   said to me,
old people and wise,   who were ancient,
that Hiltibrant was the name of my father: my name is Hadubrant.
[*Hildebrandslied*, Old High German, ninth century (?)]

Thô an theru **selb**on   stedi **ges**î**ð**os *gô*de
te **bed**u *fell*un endi   im eft te **burg** *than*an
thar te **Hier**us*al*em   **iung**aron *Crist*es
*fô*run **fag**anondi: uuas im **frâh**mod *hug*i,
uuârun im thar at themu **uuî**he   **Uuald**andes *craft*.

Then in that same place the disciples unto God
began to pray and   back to the city
where to Jerusalem   the disciples of Christ
went rejoicing: they were bold of mind,
there in that temple   were the powers of God.
[*Heliand* lines 5979–83, Old Saxon, first half of ninth century]

Þæt ic bi me **sylf**um   **secg**an *will*e,
þæt ic **hwil**e *wæs*   **Heod**eninga *scop*,
dryhtne **dyre**.   Me wæs **Deor** *nom*a.
Ahte ic **fela** *wint*ra   **folg**að *tiln*e,

holdne **hlaf**ord,   oþþæt **Heor**renda *nu,*
leoðcræftig *monn*   londryht ge*þah,*
þæt me **eorl**a *hleo*   **ær** ge*seal*de.
þæs ofer*eode,*   **þiss**es *swa* mæg!
This about myself   I wish to say,
that I long was the *scop* [court poet]   of Heodinge,
precious to my lord.   My name was Deor.
For many winters I had   a good position,
a generous lord,   until Heorrenda now,
the man strong in song,   received that right of land
which my lord had   previously granted to me.
This passed,   so shall that.
[*Deor*, Old English, tenth century]

Hljóðs bið ek *all*ar   **helg**ar *kind*ir
meiri ok **minn**i   **mǫg**u *Heim*dalar;
vildu at ek, **Valf**ǫðr,   vel fram *telj*a
forn spjǫll **fir**a,   þau er **fremst** um *man.*
Attention I ask from all the sacred people,
greater and lesser, the offspring of Heimdall;
Father of the Slain, you wished that I should declare
the ancient histories of men and gods, those which I remember
       from the first.
[*Vǫluspá* ("The Seeress's Prophecy"), Old Norse, late tenth century (?)]

Examination of these passages will show first that there are occasional lines that are metrically deficient, such as "dat *sag*etun
mi *us*ere *liuti*" in *Hildebrandslied*, which lacks alliteration. This is
hardly surprising; in most oral poetry, rhymes and meter are occasionally imperfect (just as in, say, popular songs today), and these
samples are basically oral forms set down in writing. Based on these
comparisons, we can be fairly confident that the old songs to which
Tacitus referred had this common form, and indeed we have a runic
inscription that increases our confidence, even if it is only one line.

Ek **Hle**wagastiz **Holt**ijaz   **horn**a *taw*ido
I Hlewastiz son of Holt/from Holt   made the horn
[Runic inscription on Gallehus horn, fifth century CE]

Adding this sample suggests that the form could be used for widely varying purposes. The stanza on the Rök stone and the *Hildebrandslied* narrate heroic legend that is known from multiple sources. *Deor* is elegiac, as are several poems from Old English and Old Norse. *Heliand* is an epic about the life of Christ, and Old English also has several epics in the alliterative verse from about biblical subjects, as well as short charms. Finally, *Vǫluspá* recounts myth. While it is true that nearly all mythological poetry is from Old Norse tradition written down in thirteenth-century Iceland, Wodæn/Wodan is mentioned in Old English and Old High German charms that use the alliterative verse we are discussing here, and the passage from ch. 2 of *Germania* tells us that the Germanic peoples had mythological verse. In this light, it is interesting to consider the fact that the names of the three tribal groupings, Ingaevones, Herminones, Istaevones could easily be set into an alliterative pattern.[3]

We only have mythological poetry from medieval Iceland, but we can use the heroic poems in Old English, Old High German, and Iceland to reconstruct the existence of mythological poetry in the common Germanic alliterative meter, at least for the period from the ninth century onward, and probably earlier. We can use the heroic poems because the line between gods and humans was far less sharp than it is in the major monotheistic religions that dominate much of the world today (Lindow and Schjødt 2020; Bellah 2011). From the materials already mentioned, we may cite the example of Hercules, an apparently human hero of divine origin who came to be worshipped in some contexts. In Scandinavia we may point to some kings who were apparently worshipped after their deaths, as well as

---

[3] Vowels alliterate with other vowels, and *Herminones* is probably to be understood as *Erminones*.

to the ninth-century human poet Bragi Boddason, who seems to have become a god after his death.

To judge from the heroic poems, mythological poems were likely to have been relatively short. They did not tell the whole story, which the audience presumably knew; rather they seem to have focused on the high point within a single narrative. There may have been cycles of poems on related mythological subjects, as in the extant poems about the hero Sigurðr.

In the samples cited earlier, the date of the Old Norse–Icelandic mythological poem *Vǫluspá* is given as a questionable "late tenth century (?)." This tentative dating is reached from internal evidence only: the poem seems to have both pagan and Christian elements, and the particular mixture would have been plausible during the last decades of the pagan period. That is only a guess, an informed guess to be sure, but one that is not likely to be proved given the kind of evidence we have. One may well ask how likely it is that the mythological poems like *Vǫluspá*, written down in the thirteenth century by Christian scribes, resemble the oral mythological poems that we know existed during the pagan period. Scholars have expressed widely varying opinions about this complex issue (see, for example, Gunnell and Lassen 2013 and Harris 2017), but the existence of other alliterative Germanic poetry would seem to settle the issue. While the extant mythological poems from medieval Iceland may have taken the forms they show in the manuscripts only at the time of their recording, in their subject matters and style they must resemble closely the poetry that existed during the Viking Age.

The extant poems are mostly found in two manuscripts from thirteenth-century Iceland. The longer one is usually called the *Poetic Edda*, and that is a misnomer (its contents will be discussed in chapter 3). When the manuscript was rediscovered in the seventeenth century, it was imagined to be an *Edda* by Sæmundr Sigfússon the Learned (1056–1133), parallel to that of Snorri Sturluson— which it is not. Snorri's work is in fact called *Edda* in the oldest extant manuscript (c. 1300), but it is a handbook of poetics, and that is what *Edda* probably means. The "Edda" ascribed (inaccurately) to Sæmundr is an anthology of mythological and heroic poems, nothing more. Nevertheless, for years people called this anthology *Sæmundar Edda* (the "Edda of Sæmundr"), or the "Elder Edda," since Sæmundr was a generation older than Snorri. Today only the name *Edda* has stuck, distinguished from Snorri's work by the adjective *Poetic*. Besides this one manuscript, the *Poetic Edda*, there exists a second manuscript fragment of exclusively mythological poetry, and a few additional mythological poems scattered in other manuscripts, usually manuscripts that also contain Snorri's *Edda*.

The *Poetic Edda* contains poems that are metrically identical to the alliterative poems in other Germanic languages (although they are arranged into stanzas, unlike the poems in the other languages). Alongside these were poems composed in a more elaborate set of meters based on the usual Germanic forms but different from them in that they rigorously fixed the number of syllables in a line and introduced elaborate rules for the use of rhymes and half-rhymes, as well as for the form of the foot at the end of each half-line (note that the notion of poetic feet can only apply when syllables are counted). Scholars today call this form "skaldic," based on the Old Norse noun for poet, *skáld*, and they call the others "eddic." This distinction is exaggerated and might not have made much sense to poets, but it is helpful for us. I prefer to refer to "skaldic" verse in this book as *dróttkvætt* verse, after the name of the primary metrical form (this name means literally "recited before the chieftain's retinue"). Because that form is extremely complex, it would be difficult to change even one syllable of a line in oral transmission without doing some damage to the metrical system—or at least more difficult than it would be in most of the oral poetries of the world. Accordingly, we can imagine that *dróttkvætt* poems were not changed as much in transmission as most oral poems, which vary greatly from performance to performance in most oral societies. Since we also know more or less where and when most skalds lived and worked, we can date and localize the poems that have survived, some to the Viking

Age, before the conversion to Christianity, and thus get close to Old Norse mythology as sacred narrative.

Dróttkvætt poems rely on complex metaphors called *kenningar* (singular *kenning*). The related verb is *kenna* "to teach," but the best translation of the poetic form is probably "making known." What is "made known" is a noun that, as in all metaphors, will mean something other than its usual meaning. In the kenning "tree of battle," the base word ("tree") denotes something that stands upright in the landscape. The "determinant" "of battle" tells us what kind of "tree": a warrior. Simple kennings like this are also found in Old English poetry too, but skalds could make matters more complex by substituting a kenning for the determinant. A valid battle kenning is "hail of weapons," so a warrior could be "tree of the hail of weapons." Kennings that go out to five parts are known.

Anyone who understands how kennings work could unravel a metaphor like "tree of the hail of weapons," but what about something like "thief of the liquid of the dwarfs"? This requires knowing a story, namely that Óðinn stole from a "giant" the mead of poetry,[4] which had been made by dwarfs (see chapter 1). Thus kennings are an important source, going back to the Viking Age, of our knowledge of mythology. Sometimes we get information from kennings that is completely lacking elsewhere. For example, in one kenning the poet Bragi Boddason kenned the "giant" Hrungnir with "thief of Þrúðr." Þrúðr was Þórr's daughter, and the kenning tells us that in ninth-century Norway there was probably a myth about this "giant" having abducted Þórr's daughter. We have this fact from no other source, but it does throw a different light on Þórr's duel with this "giant."

Our knowledge of kennings—indeed, of almost all older *dróttkvætt* mythological poetry—we owe to Snorri Sturluson's *Edda*. The third, longest, and, to judge from the number of manuscripts,

---

[4] The term "giant" is treated at the beginning of the next chapter.

most popular part is *Skáldskaparmál* "Language of Poetry." Besides enumerating a large number of kennings and quoting stanzas and poems in which they are found, it also has narrative sections telling the myths on which some kennings are based.

The preceding part of Snorri's *Edda*, *Gylfaginning* "Deluding of Gylfi," consists exclusively of such narratives, without reference to any didactic purpose. The narratives, that is, myths, are put in the mouths of three human wizards, "men of Asia," whom the gullible prehistoric Swedish king Gylfi visits because he has heard that their people are powerful. He poses questions, some of them openly mythological ("What is the origin of the earth?"), which the "men of Asia" answer with narratives; the topics covered do not overlap with the narratives in *Skáldskaparmál*, and between the two parts of Snorri's *Edda* nearly all of the major myths are covered. "Men of Asia" is Snorri's explanation of the word *æsir*, which means the pagan gods. For Snorri, however, they were humans wrongly considered to be gods. This theory, usually known as euhemerism, will be treated in more detail in chapter 3. It also informed the Danish history written by Saxo Grammaticus, *Gesta Danorum*, and it was almost certainly an important factor in allowing the myths, which had been transmitted for so long in oral tradition as sacred texts, to survive, in desacralized form, in the writings of medieval Christians at the edge of the known world.

In the next chapter we will take a look at the mythology, derived from the Viking Age and earlier, that we are lucky enough to be able to read in medieval manuscripts.

Chapter 1

From Cosmogony to Cosmic Eschatology

The System of Old Norse Mythology

Old Norse mythology can be said to begin, and to some extent to end, with conflict between two groups, "giants" and gods. It is important to bear in mind that the term "giants" is misleading. Although the Old Norse word most often used for this group, the plural *jǫtnar* (singular *jǫtunn*) has cognates in Old English and the modern Scandinavian languages that do refer to a being of enormous stature, there is little or no indication of such size in the mythology. The etymology of the word is uncertain, but if the best guess is correct, it originally meant something like "powerful eater" (de Vries 1961: 295–96), which might conform to the threatening nature of the group but hardly helps to define them. Numerous other terms are used for the "giants" (hereafter just giants) in Old Norse mythology, and although some scholars have sought to locate semantic distinctions among them, others have treated them as more or less synonymous (Schulz 2004: 29–52). Size is sometimes a factor with another commonly used word, *trǫll* "troll," but hardly always, and the semantics of the terms in general vary greatly depending upon the genres in which they are used. In the mythology, as mentioned, size is not a factor, since the giants interact on a more or less even footing with the gods, and both groups seek sexual partners from the other. What characterizes the giants in the mythology, besides being ugly and noisy, is primarily their opposition to the gods, the real threats they pose to the order the gods have created, and their possession of precious objects that the gods are able to obtain from them. Throughout the mythology it is a known fact that the giants will ultimately destroy the gods and the cosmos—and themselves with it; but without them there would have been no cosmos. Indeed, without the giants there would be no mythology.

There are also multiple words for the gods. The most common of these is the plural *æsir* (singular *áss*). This word, or its homonym, can mean "roof beam" or "mountain ridge," but most scholars believe that there are two separate words and that *áss* "god" derives from roots that once meant "breath" or, possibly, "king." Be that as it may, what is striking is that neither this word nor its cognates was ever used of the Christian god during or after the conversion to Christianity. Instead the word used in Old Norse was *goð*, cognate with our word *god*. Originally *goð* was a neuter noun, and in earlier poetry it is often used as a plural ("the gods"), but with the conversion to Christianity it gradually took on masculine gender and was obviously used only in the singular in Christian contexts. Other plural terms for the pagan gods include *regin* "(divine) powers," *bǫnd* "(divine) bonds," and *hǫpt* "(divine) fetters." All are neuter nouns and have no singular usage with any religious sense. Probably *bǫnd* and *hǫpt* refer to the control the gods exerted over people; in ch. 39 of *Germania* Tacitus describes a sacred grove of the Semnones, one of the tribes of Suebi:

> No one enters it until he has been bound with a chain: he puts off his freedom, and advertises in his person the might of the deity: if he chance to fall, he must not be lifted up or rise—he must writhe along the ground until he is out again: the whole superstition comes to this, that it was here where the race arose, here where dwells the god who is lord of all things; everything else is subject to him and vassal. [Petersen 1914: 319]

Giants are ancient, perhaps more ancient even than the gods. In the previous chapter I alluded to Snorri's version of the origin of gods and giants. It begins with a yawning void called Ginnungagap, in which rime (hoar frost, i.e., frozen dew) and heat meet to form life. This myth is found in *Gylfaginning*:

> And when the rime and the blowing of the warmth met so that it thawed and dripped, there was a quickening from these flowing drops due to the power of the source of the heat, and it became the form of a man, and he was given the name Ymir. [Faulkes 1987: 10]

Although Snorri situates the heat and cold in realms of north and south, the actual generation of life, as described here, fits with the volcanic landscape of Iceland, with its numerous geothermal areas with hot springs, mud pots, and the like. To the extent that such conceptions might inform Snorri's narrative, the "source of the heat" that gave life to Ymir was decidedly dangerous.

From Ymir, Snorri says, quoting an eddic verse, descend the frost-giants (i.e., the giants). This progenitor of the enemies of the gods did not procreate normally. Rather, according to Snorri:

> And it is said that when he slept, he sweated. Then there grew under his left arm a male and a female, and one of his legs begot a son with the other, and descendants come from them. These are frost-giants. [Faulkes 1987: 11]

The etymology of the name Ymir probably goes back to something like "doubled" and this could refer to his hermaphroditic reproductive strategies (and might echo Tuisto in the origin story in Tacitus's *Germania*; that name may have the root for the word "two" in it). But people hearing his name in Viking and medieval Scandinavia might have associated it in their own minds with the verb *ymja* "to whine" or "to resound" and understood it as "whiner" or more likely "noise-maker," since giants are often noisy.

The cow Auðhumla, who was mentioned in the Introduction, then emerged from drips of rime. Her milk fed Ymir, while to nurture herself, she licked salty rime stones and caused Búri, the progenitor of the gods and grandfather of Óðinn, Vili, and Vé, to emerge from them over the course of three days.

> He was beautiful in appearance, big and powerful. He begot a son called Bor. He married a wife called Bestla, daughter of the giant Bolthorn, and they had three sons. [Faulkes 1987: 11]

Thus the cow, who is to play no further role in the mythology (and whom the skalds did not use for their kennings, as far as we know), links the giants and the gods and shows just how close and intertwined the relationship between the two groups is. As one who is suckled, Ymir may be placed in an infantile role, and as one who in an albeit strange way nourishes the cow, Búri may be placed in the role of the cow's owner, and to the extent these musings have any validity, the gods are placed in a hierarchically superior position over the giants.

The reproductive methods of the two groups also establish a contrast between the monstrous and the normal (indeed, one version of st. 33 of the eddic poem *Vafþrúðnismál* "Vafthrudnir's Sayings" states that the son of Ymir's two legs had six heads). But here too there may be the establishment of hierarchical superiority. While Ymir has to content himself with an armpit for a womb and procreating legs, and his first offspring apparently had to reproduce through incestuous relationships, Borr takes as his mate a woman from another group—the daughter of a giant (Bǫlþorn, using Old Norse orthography). This pattern, of gods mating with female giants, will be repeated many times in the mythology, but the opposite will be rare and destabilizing. Margaret Clunies Ross (1994) has called this pattern "negative reciprocity," meaning that the hierarchically superior gods can take mates, and other items of value, from the giants (although as the mythology moves along, they mostly marry goddesses), while

the hierarchically inferior giants generally cannot take mates,[1] or any
other items of value, from among the gods.

Although Snorri's version of the myth of the origin of Ymir, Búri,
and the first generations of giants and gods takes place in a landscape
of the binaries south–north and heat–cold, as yet there is no cosmos.
Eddic poetry offers us two cosmogonies. In one, the sons of Burr
(that is, Óðinn, Vili, and Vé) "brought up the land-surface" (*Vǫluspá*
st. 4). In this poem, the earth will sink into the sea at the end of the
mythic present time, so it is possible that the sons of Burr lifted it up
out of the sea. We have no more information about this version of
cosmogony. On the other hand, the second version occurs in several sources. In the eddic poem *Vafþrúðnismál*, a contest of wisdom
between Óðinn and the giant Vafþrúðnir, Óðinn asks Vafþrúðnir
about the origin of the cosmos. This is the giant's response:

> "From Ymir's flesh the earth was shaped,
> and the mountains from his bones;
> the sky from the skull of the frost-cold giant,
> and the sea from his blood." [*Vafþrúðnismál* st. 21]

The premise of the eddic poem *Grímnismál* "Grimnir's Sayings"
is that Óðinn has been hung over a fire in the hall of the human king
Geirrøðr, where he has an ecstatic vision. He sees the abodes of the
gods and then begins to recount additional information about the
cosmos. Then Óðinn says:

> "From Ymir's flesh the earth was made,
> and from his blood, the sea,
> mountains from his bones, trees from his hair,
> and from his skull, the sky.

---

[1] The eddic poem *Hymiskviða* "Hymir's Song" appears to offer an exception, in that
it seems to present the giant Hymir as the father of the god Týr. This matter is treated in
chapter 2.

And from his eyelashes the cheerful gods
made Midgard for men's sons;
and from his brain the hard-tempered clouds
were all created." [*Grímnismál* st. 40–41]

As st. 41 states, humans live in "Midgard," Old Norse Miðgarðr "central enclosure." The gods live in Ásgarðr "divine enclosure." Both of these nouns are grammatically singular. Oppsed to these one does find Útgarðr "outer enclosure" once, but it probably "should not be considered an old or genuine concept" (Vikstrand 2006: 356). The usual term for the abode of the giants is Jǫtunheimar "giant lands." The plural perhaps indicates multiple locations on the periphery of the cosmos, as would be appropriate both for monstrous beings and for a hierarchically inferior society. The opposition between the center, where gods and humans live, and the periphery, where the giants live, is a cosmic indication of the opposition between the groups. In recognition of the fact, I shall use the form "Giantlands" in this book.

It was the gods who made Miðgarðr for humans. This brings humans into the system as the clients of the gods, which is what we would expect of myths as sacred texts. But how exactly did the gods make Miðgarðr out of Ymir's eyelashes? Snorri has the answer: Óðinn, Vili, and Vé killed him and fashioned the cosmos out of his body parts. What this means is that the sons of Borr killed a maternal relative. How many links there might have been between the armpit children and six-headed son of Ymir's legs is beyond recovery, but it cannot have been many. If Bǫlþorn was himself one of Ymir's monstrously conceived offspring, the gods killed their mother's grandfather.

The consequences of this killing are contradictory. On the one hand, killing the first giant was a creative act in that it enabled the construction of the cosmos, and therefore it would seem that whenever a god killed a giant, he engaged symbolically in a creative act, re-creating, as it were, the cosmos. On the other hand, killing the first giant was a killing within a family. Thus the very existence of the cosmos was deeply fraught, for the cosmos was built upon a murder within a family. Although it might perhaps be argued that the killing of Ymir was a sacrificial act, perhaps even a voluntary one, what we know about human sacrifice in Viking Age religion is that the victims were outside the family and indeed outside society, either defeated warriors or persons without status, such as slaves.

Various sources agree that the cosmos had a sacred center, where there was a sacred ash tree called Yggdrasill, which appears to mean "Óðinn's steed," and a sacred well associated with wisdom and fate. The roots of the tree reach to and therefore conjoin various parts of the cosmos. However, just as the cosmos is built on a crime, so the tree that symbolizes the unity of the cosmos is deeply beset. Óðinn's vision of the cosmos in *Grímnismál* includes these stanzas:

> "There are four harts too, who browse on its shoots,
> with their necks tilted back;
> Dain and Dvalin,
> Duneyr and Durathror.

> More serpents lie under Yggdrasill's ash
> than any numbskull fool can imagine:
> Goin and Moin, they are Grafvitnir's sons,
> Grabak and Grafvollud,
> Ofnir and Svafnir I think for ever will
> erode the tree's branches.

> Yggdrasill's ash suffers agony
> more than men know:
> a stag nibbles it above, but at its side it's decaying,
> and Nidhogg rends it beneath." [*Grímnismál* st. 33–35]

As these stanzas show, Old Norse mythology was a mythology of names. To some degree this derives from, or is consistent with, the fact that Old Norse poetry is a poetry of nouns. Knowing all these names, and the obscure nouns of poetry, and being able to unravel kennings, were important aspects of wisdom. But here the names, or at least some of them, help highlight the trouble the tree is in. Ursula Dronke rendered the names of st. 33 (Dáinn, etc.) as "Dead One and Dawdling One, Downy Beach and Door Stubborn" and those of 34 as "Soil Worm and Heath Worm—they are the sons of Grave Wolf—Grey Back and Grave Digger, Twister and Killer" (Dronke 2011: 120). As for Níðhǫggr, Dronke's "Malice Striker" is another eloquent translation. Níðhǫggr is likely to be a snake or dragon.

Once the cosmos was created from the body of Ymir, there was still work to do.

> From the south, Sun, companion of the moon,
> threw her right hand round the sky's edge;
> Sun did not know where she had her hall,
> the stars did not know where they had their stations,
> the moon did not know what might he had.
>
> Then all the Powers went to the thrones of fate,
> the sacrosanct gods, and considered this:
> to night and her children they gave names,
> morning they named and midday,
> afternoon and evening, to reckon up in years. [*Vǫluspá* st. 5–6]

Since no source has the gods creating the sun and moon (in *Gylfaginning* Snorri says they derive from sparks where hot and cold met, and other sources are silent), they must be regarded as gods, or at least as parallel to the gods. Indeed, in his vision in *Grímnismál*, Óðinn refers to the sun as "the shining goddess" (st. 38 and 39), and Snorri states explicitly in *Gylfaginning* that Sól ("sun") is a goddess. In these stanzas from *Grímnimsál*, and the one preceding it, Óðinn tells how the sun moves through the sky, how she is equipped, and how two wolves pursue her (wolves are aligned with the giants, as will become apparent below). The motion of the sun by means of a conveyance appears to be present on picture stones from Gotland from roughly the third to the sixth centuries CE, as is seen in figure 1.1.

The sun may be female and the moon male because those are the grammatical genders of the two nouns. As for the stars, it is difficult

FIGURE 1.1 Picture stone from Sanda, Gotland, dated to the fifth century, one of the many Gotlandic picture stones containing aspects of a solar myth: the sun atop the stone with rising and setting suns beneath. It is likely that the ship was conceived as carrying the sun out of and back into darkness each day. Photo: Anders Andrén.

for us today, living with electric lights in cities and towns, to imagine the impact they must have had in earlier times. Nevertheless, it is far from clear how the celestial bodies interact with Old Norse mythology; and what is important in the cosmogony is that the gods were able to create order for them, in order to enable time reckoning—presumably the power that the moon did not know he had.

After ordering nature, the gods created culture. This they did by creating tools, especially for metalwork.

> The Æsir met on Idavoll Plain,
> high they built altars and temples;
> they set up their forges, smithed precious things,
> shaped tongs and made tools. [*Vǫluspá* st. 7]

The golden age of the gods did not last long.

> They played chequers in the meadow, they were merry,
> they did not lack for gold at all,
> until three ogre-girls came,
> all-powerful women, out of Giant-land. [*Vǫluspá* st. 8]

Who exactly these "ogre-girls" (female giants) are, and how they disrupted the merry life of the gods, is not spelled out. We can, however, note that they seem to have arrived of their own accord and uninvited, rather than as sexual conquests brought back from Giantlands by the gods. On a later occasion, the giantess Skaði arrived in Ásgarðr to seek compensation for the gods' killing of her father Þjazi. Whether that myth is analogous to the disruption of the gods' early bliss or not, it is not difficult to assume that the gods' killing of the progenitor of the race of giants, for whatever purpose, would lead sooner or later to enmity between the two groups, and the three giant girls seem to have activated that enmity.

In *Vǫluspá* the gods' reaction to the incursion is in an extremely difficult passage, but it clearly has to do with dwarfs. The usual

understanding is that the gods choose to create dwarfs at this point,
but it is not impossible to read one of the two eddic manuscripts, and
versions cited by Snorri, as saying instead that the dwarfs are to create
a troop or troops. In Old Norse mythology, dwarfs constitute an exclusively male group of artisanal craftsmen who live in stones and the
earth. Just as there is no indication that the giants are large, so there
is no indication that dwarfs are small. Dwarfs for the most part do
not participate in the struggle between gods and giants, except insofar as they produce precious objects for the gods. If the difficult
lines in Vǫluspá st. 9 tell us that the gods created dwarfs at this point,
it might be because their own ability to smith precious things had
been compromised. If the dwarfs were to create troops or a troop, the
reference might be to "manlike figures" alluded to in st. 10:

> There Motsognir became most famous of
> all dwarfs, and Durin next;
> many manlike figures the dwarfs made,
> out of the earth, as Durin recounted.[2]

Although these could also be descendants of the first dwarfs, the
idea that they are proto-humans makes more sense to me because
of what ensues.

Following a lengthy catalogue of dwarf names, the poet returns
to the theme of creation:

> Until three gods, strong and loving,
> came from out of that company;
> they found on land capable of little,
> Ash and Embla, lacking in fate.

---

[2] Larrington's translation follows the text in the *Poetic Edda*. In the other manuscript
of eddic poetry, Motsógnir and Durinn create "many manlike figures, dwarfs in the earth."
The stanza is found before, not after, the catalogue of dwarf-names, so this version of the
poem represents a significantly different variant, one that will not accord with the interpretation I put forth here. In *Gylfaginning*, Snorri cites the half-stanza in question in a form that
accords with neither of the other two.

> Breath they had not, spirit they had not,
> blood nor bearing nor fresh complexions;
> breath gave Odin, spirit gave Hænir,
> blood gave Lodur, and fresh complexions. [*Vǫluspá* st. 17–18]

In *Gylfaginning* Snorri explains that Askr (lit. "ash-tree," a masculine noun and therefore to be taken as male here) and Embla (a feminine noun and therefore female) were blocks of wood by the shore, which would accord with the "manlike figures" of *Vǫluspá* st. 10. Lacking life, they are indeed "capable of little." The nouns enumerating the requirements for animation set forth in *Vǫluspá* st. 18 pose numerous semantic challenges, and Carolyne Larrington's brave attempt at translation just cited is as good as any. Snorri adds other aspects, such as sight and hearing.

The "strong and loving gods" who animate the "manlike figures" are Óðinn, whom we have already met in the Introduction; Hœnir, a relatively obscure figure often seen in triads with Óðinn; and Lóðurr, an utterly unknown figure. Based on the existence of a traveling triad Óðinn-Hœnir-Loki, some scholars assume that Lóðurr may be a name for Loki. According to Snorri, the triad that animated the blocks of wood were the sons of Borr, that is, Óðinn, Vili, and Vé. These variant readings are fully consistent with the mythology of an oral religion.

"Lacking in fate" indicates that fate is a requirement for human life, and it is likely that st. 20 of *Vǫluspá* addresses this issue (st. 19 describes the world tree, which stands over the well of fate; the order of 19 and 20 is reversed in one of the two eddic manuscripts, putting the stanza that follows here directly after the two just cited.).

> From there came girls, knowing a great deal,
> three from the lake standing under the tree;
> Urd one is called, Verdandi another—
> they carved on a wooden slip—Skuld the third;
> they laid down laws, they chose lives
> for the sons of men, the fates of men. [*Vǫluspá* st. 20]

The name of the middle girl, Verðandi, is identical with the present participle of the verb *verða* "become," and the name Urðr contains the root of the past tense of that verb; these names might thus mean something like "Became" and "Becoming," to put them in chronological order. The name Skuld is identical with the noun meaning "debt," which itself is derived from the root of the auxiliary verb *skulu* "should" and might therefore imply something to happen in the future.

Most scholars assume that these three girls are the fate beings known as norns (Old Norse *nornir*, a feminine plural noun). Conceptions of them vary somewhat in the sources, but they often seem to be present at childbirth to endow the child with the fate he or she will live out as an adult, fate being for the most part understood as focused on the hour and manner of death. This trope was quite productive in heroic legend. The exact relationship between the norns and the gods is difficult to pin down, since the gods have fates too, and there is no strong evidence of worship of the norns.

This anthropogony illustrates a few points about the complexity of Old Norse mythology as sacred narratives. Humans owe their lives to a trio of gods, but other powerful non-human beings were involved as well: the dwarfs to fashion the "manlike figures" (at least in one version of *Vǫluspá*) and the norns to endow fate.

The conceptual world of the Viking Age religion from which Old Norse mythology derives was thus complex. Besides gods, giants, dwarfs, and norns, there were *álfar* (masc. plur.; sing *álfr*), cognate with English elfs but a divine group; and *dísir* (fem. plur.; sing. *dís*), probably "ladies," who intersected with human lives in various ways having to do with fate and death and who were the object of cult. Humans, however, play only a very small role in the mythology, as we shall see.

A few additional myths describe how the mythological world got to be the way it is. Of these the most important comprised a war between two groups of gods, the Æsir and the Vanir. The original meaning of this latter word is disputed, but subsequent to the war all gods could be called Æsir and only a few Vanir.

Vǫluspá contains several stanzas about the beginning and early course of the war:

> She remembers the first war in the world,
> when they struck Gullveig with spears
> and in the High-One's hall they burned her;
> three times they burned her, three times she was reborn,
> over and over, yet she lives still.
>
> Bright One they called her, wherever she came to houses,
> the seer with pleasing prophecies, she practiced spirit-magic;
> she knew *seid*, *seid* she performed as she liked,
> she was always a wicked woman's favourite.
>
> Then all the Powers went to the thrones of fate,
> the sacrosanct gods, and considered this:
> whether the Æsir should yield the tribute
> or whether all the gods should share sacrificial feasts.
>
> Odin hurled a spear, sped it into the host;
> that was war still, the first in the world;
> the wooden rampart of the Æsir's stronghold was wrecked;
> the Vanir, with a war-spell, kept on trampling the plain.
> [*Vǫluspá* st. 22–25][3]

The High-One is Óðinn. The names of the woman who, like the three giant girls, invaded the home of the gods and disrupted their society are found only here. *Gullveig* looks as though it should be a simple compound meaning "gold-drink," hardly a normal name, and "Bright One" (Old Norse *Heiðr*) is not a normal name either. Many scholars associate her with the figure who, in the mythology

---

[3] These stanzas are numbered 21–24 in most editions and translations.

at least, is the most important of the Vanir, namely the goddess Freyja. According to the mythology she has a great many names (indeed, Freyja means just "lady"), and she is closely associated with magic, particularly the kind of magic called *seiðr*, which she taught to the Æsir. *Seiðr* could be used to see the future, but it could also be used aggressively against other people, and in the mythology it is said to be so shameful that for a man rather than a woman to practice it is to risk his reputation. Scholars have long considered the extent to which this form of magic may have been related to shamanism, especially that of the Sámi, the northern neighbors of the Scandinavians. As a small footnote here, shamans' bodies often appear lifeless while they are off on spirit journeys, although of course they are not normally stabbed or burned, as is Gullveig/Heiðr.

The last two of the four stanzas from *Vǫluspá* just cited have the disruption of Gullveig/Heiðr (Freyja?) escalate into a full-scale war, which is left unresolved. However, Snorri Sturluson explained how it ended, both in the *Skáldskaparmál* section of his *Edda* and in ch. 4 of *Ynglinga saga*, the first saga in his compilation of sagas about Norwegian kings that bears the title *Heimskringla*. There we learn that Óðinn, here understood as a human king leading a migration of his people from Troy to Sweden (see chapter 3), made war against another people, the Vanir. When neither side could gain the upper hand, they agreed upon a truce. The mechanism of the truce was an exchange of "hostages"—so designated because they are pledges of good faith rather than kidnap victims who can be useful in hostile negotiation—as follows: from the Vanir to the Æsir the wealthy Njǫrðr, his son Freyr, and the wise Kvasir; from the Æsir to the Vanir the tall and handsome Hœnir and the wise Mímir. The Vanir appointed Hœnir a chieftain, but when they learned that he was unable to function without the counsel of Mímir, they beheaded Mímir and sent the head to the Æsir. Óðinn embalmed it and it became a valuable source of wisdom for him. Óðinn appointed Njǫrðr and

Freyr as priests, and Freyja too presided over cult. Freyr and Freyja were the offspring of Njǫrðr and his sister, and the Æsir banned such incestuous unions.

This account leaves Kvasir dangling, but he plays a large role in the aftermath of the war in the version of the story in *Skáldskaparmál*. There we read that the two divine groups spat into a vat, and out of this was created Kvasir; "he was so wise that no one could ask him any questions to which he did not know the answers" (Faulkes 1987: 62). He traveled about dispensing wisdom but was killed by two dwarfs who made from his blood a mead that made of whoever drank from it a poet or scholar. They were, however, forced to give the mead to a giant, Suttungr, whose mother they had killed (ordinarily dwarfs do not engage so consistently in homicide). Óðinn stole the mead from the giant by entering, in the form of a snake, the mountain in which Suttungr lived and seducing or raping the giant's daughter, Gunnlǫð, who allowed him to drink some of it. He flew back to Ásgarðr pursued by Suttungr, both in the form of eagles, and spat most of it safely into vats, although a bit leaked out of his rear end and became the share of trivial poets.

The Vanir differ from the Æsir in several important ways, of which their incestuous unions are only one symbolic expression. Most scholars accept that the name of Njǫrðr, the wealthy hostage sent to the Æsir and the father of Freyr and Freyja, is identical to that of a goddess Nerthus "or Mother Earth" described by Tacitus in *Germania* ch. 40. During a ritual she is transported about in a wagon, and while the procession is going on: "They make no war, take no arms: every weapon is put away; peace and quiet are then, and then alone, known and loved" (Petersen 1914: 321). The difference in the sex of Nerthus and Njǫrðr could have to do with the incest of the Vanir, or with variation in time and space, or even, if implausibly, with the fact that feminine nouns of the grammatical class in which Nerthus/Njǫrðr is found ceased to exist in early Old Norse.

Be that as it may, here is how Snorri describes Freyr in *Gylfaginning*:

Freyr is the most glorious of the Æsir. He is ruler of rain and sun-shine and thus of the produce of the earth, and it is good to pray to him for prosperity and peace. He also rules over the wealth of men. [Faulkes 1987: 24]

The Vanir are thus fertility gods, and the war and settlement show how such gods came to be incorporated with the gods of warfare and battle.[4] It is important to recall, too, that the outcome of the set-tlement between Æsir and Vanir was not only the incorporation of the two groups, but also the creation of the mead of poetry. This substance is what made wisdom and memory possible, since both were encoded in verse.

Despite the incorporation of the two groups, it seems that the Vanir were hierarchically inferior to the original Æsir, since they take their wives not from that group but from the giants. Njǫrðr has a brief and disastrous marriage to Skaði, a giantess whose name is a masculine noun meaning "damage." The marriage came about after the gods had killed Skaði's father and she appeared armed and dan-gerous to demand compensation. The gods let her choose a husband from among them but allowed her to see only their feet, and she chose Njǫrðr instead of the one she had hoped for, namely Baldr. As for Freyr, he spied the shoulders of a woman in Giantlands and became so enamored that he fell sick. His servant was dispatched to Giantlands to woo the woman on Freyr's behalf and succeeded only through curses and threats. The poem that tells this myth, *Skírnismál* ("Skírnir's sayings;" an alternate and more descriptive

---

[4] The idea that the myth might reflect some kind of actual war between adherents of a warlike religion and a fertility religion has been regarded by most scholars as unlikely ever since Georges Dumézil showed its function in structuralist terms across various Indo-European mythologies. See further Dumézil (1973) and chapter 4, below.

title is *Fǫr Skírnis* "Skírnir's Journey"), ends with the marriage not yet consummated: Freyr is to wait nine nights for the wedding and is distraught. Thus it could be said that neither Njǫrðr nor Freyr is lucky in love.

Other myths of origin involve the incorporation of Loki with the gods and the binding of his monstrous children. Loki was the son of a giant and therefore a giant according to the patrilineal system of kinship reckoning that characterizes the mythology (this represented a conceptual simplification, since as far as we can tell, kinship was reckoned bilaterally in early Scandinavian society). To make matters worse, his mother may have been a goddess, and thus his parentage would represent the kind of destabilizing reproduction mentioned in the beginning of this chapter. And yet, Snorri tells us in *Gylfaginning* that Loki was "also reckoned among the Æsir" (Faulkes 1987: 26), which is curious not only given his parentage but also given the fact that there is no evidence that Loki was ever worshipped as a god. The explanation for this enigma appears to be set forth in st. 9 of the poem *Lokasenna* "Loki's Quarrel," in which Loki arrives as an uninvited guest at a feast of the gods. At first denied entry, he appeals to Óðinn:

> "Do you remember, Odin, when in bygone days
> we blended our blood together?
> You said you'd never imbibe beer
> unless it were brought to both of us." [*Lokasenna* st. 9]

Blending blood together refers to an oath of blood-brotherhood, a ritual that we see a few times in the Old Norse sources. Participants would mix their blood, vow an oath, and in some cases go under a piece of turf cut from but still attached to the earth, probably thus enacting a symbolic death and rebirth. The result was not so much that the blood-brothers would, like Óðinn and Loki, drink together, as that each would avenge the other in the way that a brother would. Before the strong central authority of the Nordic kingdoms evolved,

society was of the kind sometimes called "self-help," in which
bloodfeud was a central mechanism of dispute resolution. When a
person was killed, it fell to his nearest blood-relative—son, father,
brother—to seek compensation or vengeance. The oath of blood-
brotherhood taken by Óðinn and Loki "in bygone days" is the only
such oath in the mythology. While we have very little information
about it, from Óðinn's perspective it might perhaps be seen as a way
to neutralize the threat of Loki and his children.

According to Snorri in *Gylfaginning* (Faulkes 1987: 26), Loki
had three children with the giantess Angrboða in Giantlands,
that is, before he had joined the gods: the wolf Fenrir (sometimes called Fenris-wolf), Jǫrmungandr the World Serpent,[5]
and a daughter Hel. That a wolf and a serpent can result from the
breeding of giants suggests again just how dangerous they are. The
gods foresaw the threats, and Óðinn cast the serpent into the sea,
where he surrounds the earth.[6] Hel he threw down into the world
of the dead, over which she presides. Neutralizing the wolf proved
more difficult. When the gods bound him, he simply burst the
fetters with his great strength. So the gods got a magic fetter from
some dwarfs, but the wolf was suspicious because it appeared to
be harmless. He only agreed to be bound with it if one of the gods
would put a hand in his mouth "as a pledge that this is done in
good faith." Týr agreed:

> And now when the wolf kicked, the band grew harder, and the
> harder he struggled, the tougher became the band. Then they all
> laughed except for Tyr. He lost his hand. [Faulkes 19897: 29]

---

[5] In Old Norse the beast is called *Miðgarðsormr* "serpent of Miðgarðr," and thus sometimes in English "Midgard serpent." I choose the designation "World Serpent" because
the beast encircles the earth, conceived of as a disk surrounded by an ocean. The name
Jǫrmungandr is discussed briefly in the next chapter.

[6] The cosmology implied here is that the earth is wholly surrounded by the sea. Although
it is consistent with medieval Christian thinking, early kennings suggest that it also
characterized the world view of pre-Christian Scandinavia.

The pledge is of course false, since the binding was done in bad faith. Thus the gods are oath-breakers, and Týr is permanently maimed.

Loki is definitely a prime motor within the mythology, and the gods owe many of their most precious objects to his actions, even when such actions are ambiguous or worse. For example, one myth that Snorri recounts in *Skáldksaparmál* in his *Edda* begins when "for love of mischief" (Faulkes 1987: 96) Loki had cut off all the hair of Sif, the wife of Þórr. That is a peculiar thing to have done, and the practical result would be to make it impossible to tell Sif's marital status, since unmarried and married women wore their hair differently. And how did Loki get close enough to her to cut off her hair? Were they lovers? Did he steal into her bedroom while she slept? No one knows. In any case, the result of this mischievous or malicious act was that Þórr threatened to break every bone in Loki's body until Loki promised to get Sif some new hair that would grow into gold. This he had some dwarfs make, and they also made a ship, Skíðblaðnir, that always has a favorable wind and can be folded up; it went to Freyr according to Snorri, although another source makes it Óðinn's. The third object is the spear Gungnir, which is "never stopped in its thrust" (Faulkes 1987: 97), and goes to Óðinn. "Then Loki wagered his head with a dwarf called Brokk on whether his brother Eitri would make three precious things as good as these were" (Faulkes 1987: 96). In the form of a fly biting Brokkr while he works the bellows, Loki tries to interfere with the smithing, but he only succeeds in slightly marring the third object. The three that Eitri makes are a boar with golden bristles that goes to Freyr; the golden ring Draupnir, which makes copies of itself (and is therefore a wealth machine) and goes to Óðinn; and the hammer Mjǫllnir, which goes to Þórr. Despite the short handle, caused by Loki's interference with Brokkr working the bellows, Mjǫllnir is a weapon that will never miss a target, even when thrown, and when thrown it will return to Þórr's hand. Numerous miniature hammers have been uncovered by archaeologists; these were apparently worn as amulets around the neck (see figure 1.2 for an example).

FIGURE 1.2 A Þórr's hammer from Skåne, Sweden (SHM 9822:106659). Note the prominent eyes. Photo: Gabriel Hildebrand, Statens Historiska Museum, Stockholm.

These are indeed more precious objects than the first three, and when Brokkr finally captures Loki, with Þórr's help, Loki tells him that he cannot be beheaded because he wagered only his head, not his neck. The dwarf then stitches Loki's lips together. Although there exists an image of a man with lips apparently sewn shut and thus presumably Loki (figure 1.3), this motif never reappears, and it never interferes with Loki's ability to speak—indeed, to speak cleverly—which is at the core of the identity of this ambiguous mythological figure.

Besides thus providing the major gods with their characteristic accoutrements, according to another myth told in full in *Gylfaginning* Loki also contributed to the building of the fortification of Ásgarðr and in so doing saved Freyja and the sun and moon. They were

FIGURE 1.3 Protection stone for a bellows found in Snaptun in central Jylland (Nationalmuseet no. FHM72A). Photo: Lennart Larsen, Nationalmuseet, København.

the payment to be given to the builder with whom the gods had contracted, thinking that since no one was to help him, he would never complete the project on schedule and would thus forfeit the payment. But he asked to be able to use his stallion, Svaðilfœri, to help with the work, and "It was Loki that was responsible for this being granted him" (Faulkes 1987: 35). When it became apparent that, with the stallion's help, the builder would complete the project on schedule, the gods confronted Loki. Loki turned himself into a mare and seduced Svaðilfœri, effectively putting a stop to the project just days from completion. When the builder went into a rage the gods realized the obvious: the builder was a giant, and they called on Þórr to kill him. Subsequently Loki gave birth to a foal, Óðinn's eight-legged horse Sleipnir. Figure 1.4, from the island of Gotland

FIGURE 1.4 Picture stone from Tjängvide in Alskog on Gotland, dated to the ninth century (SHM 4171:108203). This image is from the top panel of the stone. Photo: Statens Historiska Museum, Stockholm.

off the east coast of Sweden, almost certainly portrays Óðinn on Sleipnir, being greeted by a woman with a drinking horn, perhaps in front of Óðinn's Valhǫll.

Those who heard this last part of the myth in pre-Christian times would have understood it not as an amusing story about a tricky schemer but rather as a permanently damaging feature of Loki. In the Old Norse world, men guarded their reputations carefully. Accusations of cowardice were highly charged, and accusations about a man's sexuality were "fully chargeable offenses"—we would say serious felonies. The Old Norwegian Gulaþing (the district around Bergen) law cites examples of these "fully chargeable offenses."

One is if a man says to another that he has given birth to a child. A second is if a man says of another that he is *sannsorðinn* (demonstrably used sexually by another man). The third is if he compares him to a mare, or calls him a bitch or a harlot, or compares him with the female of any kind of animal. [Meulengracht Sørensen 1983: 16]

According to the Old Icelandic law called *Grágás*, a man had a right to kill another man who used certain words about him in connection with such accusations. So Loki's sexuality is certainly deeply ambiguous. According to another myth, part of Skaði's compensation, mentioned earlier, was that the gods were to make her laugh. This Loki achieved by tying one end of a rope around his testicles and the other to the beard of a goat; both bleated as Loki fell into Skaði's lap, and she laughed. This too cannot have enhanced Loki's reputation.

The other god with ambiguous sexuality is Loki's blood-brother Óðinn. In *Lokasenna* st. 21–24 they engage in this dialogue, exchanging accusations beginning with Loki's hint of Óðinn's rewarding of cowardice but moving on to what the law would have called fully chargeable offenses, which neither of them denies. Loki has just insulted Gefjon, one of the goddesses.

> *Odin said:*
> "Mad you are, Loki, and out of your wits,
> when you make Gefion angry with you,
> for I think she knows all the fate of the world,
> as clearly as I myself."

> *Loki said:*
> "Be silent, Odin, you could never
> apportion war-fortune among men;
> often you've given what you shouldn't have given,
> victory, to the faint-hearted."

> *Odin said:*
> "You know, if I gave what I shouldn't have given,
> victory, to the faint-hearted,

yet eight winters you were, beneath the earth,
a milchcow and a woman,
and there you bore children,
and that I thought the hallmark of a pervert."

Loki said:
"But you, they say, practiced *seid* on Samsey,
and you beat on the drum as seeresses do,
in the likeness of a wizard you journeyed over mankind,
and that I thought the hallmark of a pervert."

The word translated "pervert" here is one of the words that justify a man to slay another who uses it against him. Óðinn's insults correspond to what the Gulaþing law expressly prohibits; Loki's accusation against Óðinn is for using *seiðr*, the form of magic discussed earlier.

Loki's ambivalence shows in his roles in the numerous myths in which he participates. Often, as in the story of the building of the wall around Ásgarðr, he gets the gods in trouble and then helps them get out it. Sometimes he travels with other gods, both in the triad Óðinn-Hœnir-Loki and also as a companion to Þórr. But as the world nears and comes to its end, he acts as their enemy.

When Óðinn acquires the mead of poetry, we see one of the common types of myth in the "mythic present": a myth of acquisition. The giants have something of value, and the gods take it from them and put it to use. In most of these acquisition myths the giants do not use the precious object, whether from ignorance of its value and usage or from simple disinterest. In another acquisition myth, the gods need a kettle to brew beer, and Þórr, accompanied by Týr, travels to visit the giant Hymir to get a kettle from him; the myth is told in the eddic poem *Hymiskviða* "Hymir's Poem" and by Snorri in *Gylfaginning*. (Embedded in this myth complex is a version of Þórr's fishing up of the World Serpent, which is the subject of the next chapter.) According to *Hymiskviða*, Týr is the son of the giant

Hymir and a goddess mother (for an alternative reading, see the next chapter), which violates the usual process of negative reciprocity and may explain why Hymir is such a fierce and powerful enemy; his powerful gaze causes a pillar to shatter. Þórr gets the kettle by meeting a challenge set by the giant to smash a goblet. It falls unharmed to the ground when he hurls it at a pillar, but shatters when, as Hymir's wife advises, Þórr smashes it against the giant's skull. As a second test, the gods must lift the kettle. Týr cannot budge it, but Þórr succeeds and carries it off.

> They had gone a long way
> when Odin's son looked once behind him;
> he saw from the boulder-heaps,
> from the east with Hymir
> a many-headed army marching along.
>
> He lifted from his shoulders the outstanding cauldron,
> he swung Miollnir before him, keen to kill,
> and he struck down all the lava-whales. [*Hymiskviða* st. 35–36]

The many-headed army in st. 35 is probably to be understood as an army of many-headed beings, as would accord with some of the giants we have already met. The kenning for giants in st. 36, "lava-whales," presents the giants as enormous creatures of the volcanic Icelandic landscape.

Perhaps more common than acquisition myths are myths of reacquisition. Loki initiates several of these. In one, found both in a *dróttkvætt* poem, *Haustlǫng* "Autumn-long" (perhaps referring to the time of composition), an ekphrasis of the decorations on a shield composed by the later ninth-century Norwegian poet Þjóðólfr ór Hvini, and also in a prose summary in *Skáldskaparmál*, Loki is traveling with Óðinn and Hœnir when they find themselves unable to cook an ox. Snorri tells us that the cause is an eagle (actually the giant Þjazi) perched above them, and they offer to share with him. However, he takes most of the ox. In anger, Loki whacks the eagle with a pole, but the pole sticks to the eagle, who flies off, with Loki attached "so that he was about to be torn apart" (*Haustlǫng* st. 8; Clunies Ross 2017d: 443). The giant extracts from Loki, "pain-crazed" (st. 9; Clunies Ross 2017d: 444), a promise to bring to him the goddess Iðunn along with her apples that keep the gods forever young. The parallel with the demand of the giant builder of the wall around Ásgarðr for Freyja, the sun, and the moon should be obvious, but in this case the giant briefly gets what he demanded. When the gods grow old and gray, they bind Loki, who agrees to retrieve Iðunn and the apples. This he does in the form of a hawk—according to Snorri he changes Iðunn into a nut and holds her in his beak, but Þjóðólfr just says that he used magic—and Þjazi pursues him in eagle form. In st. 13, Þjóðólfr describes how Þjazi died in a crash caused when his feathers were singed in a fire that the gods had kindled, and this subsequently led to the marriage of his daughter Skaði to Njǫrðr, discussed earlier.

> Shafts quickly began to burn, which the mighty powers had shaved, and the son of the wooer of Greip <giantess> [GIANT > = Þjazi] is scorched; there was a swerve in his course. [st. 13; ed. Clunies Ross 2017d: 451].[7]

Perhaps the most famous myth of reacquisition is found only in an eddic poem, *Þrymskviða* "Thrym's Poem," which many readers find bawdy and comic. It opens with Þórr in a rage because his hammer Mjǫllnir has been stolen. Although there is no indication that Loki is involved, Þórr calls on him to find out what has happened. Borrowing Freyja's feather shape, he flies off to Giantlands, where the giant Þrymr (a noun meaning "loud noise") boasts that he has

---

[7] For the conventions used in the translations of *dróttkvætt* poetry, see the Preface.

the hammer and the price for its return—this will sound familiar—
is Freyja as his bride (at least he leaves the sun and moon and the
gods' apples of youth alone). Freyja quite naturally will have nothing
to do with such a solution, so in a meeting to discuss the crisis wise
Heimdallr suggests that Þórr should impersonate Freyja:

> "Let's tie on Thor a bridal head-dress,
> let him wear the great necklace of the Brisings.
>
> Let keys jingle by his side
> and women's clothing fall down over his knees,
> and on his breast display jewels,
> and we'll put a pointed head-dress properly on his head!"
> [Þrymskviða st. 15–16]

The necklace of the Brisings (Old Norse Brísingamen) is Freyja's
greatest jewel, and keys are the sign of a married woman who is head
of household.

Þórr reacts as any self-respecting male would in a world of
hyper-masculinity.

> Then said Thor, the vigorous god:
> "The Æsir will call me perverse,
> if I let you tie a bridal head-dress on me." [Þrymskviða st. 17]

He is right, of course, but without the hammer, "The giants will be
settling in Asgard," as Loki puts it in st. 18. In st. 20 Loki further
muddies the sexual waters; when uttering, "We two shall drive to
Giant-land," he uses a form of the numeral "two" that must indicate
one male and one female, leaving open which of them he thinks will
be which.

In the home of Þrymr, Þórr has trouble controlling his mas-
sive appetite and thirst, but Loki explains: "Freyja ate nothing for
eight nights, so madly eager was she to come to Giant-land" (st. 26).

Trying to sneak a kiss, the giant lifts Freyja's veil and is terrified by the burning eyes he sees below it. Again Loki has an explanation, plausible at least to the giant: "Freyja did not sleep for eight nights, so madly eager was she to come to Giant-land" (st. 28). The giant orders Mjǫllnir to be brought in to consecrate the bride and placed on "her" lap. Þorr snatches it up and kills all the giants.

So Þórr got his hammer back, but at what cost? In order to regain the weapon that keeps the world of gods and humans safe from the giants, Þórr has to sacrifice, or at least put at risk, his masculine honor. The burlesque of the plot notwithstanding, the crisis was very real, and it shows just how close the ongoing struggle between the gods and giants is and how large the stakes are. Although some scholars have argued that the poem is late, the theft of the thunder-god's weapon is a tale pattern known from throughout the North, and the plot is fully consistent with the rest of the mythology as we know it. Even if the language of the poem and some of its details are late, the myth is likely to be old and important.

In most of these myths of acquisition or reacquisition, one or more giants die at the hands of the gods at the end of the narrative. Since a giant-slaying replicates the killing of Ymir, which enabled the creation of the cosmos, the acquisition or reacquisition must be regarded symbolically as a creative act, re-enacting the creation of the cosmos, but because the giant's killing replicates a murder within a family, the acquisition or reacquisition is fraught.

Another important myth of acquisition is of a completely different order, namely Óðinn's self-sacrifice, through which he obtains occult wisdom, his weapon in the ongoing struggle with the giants. This myth is central to the mythology of Óðinn. It is told in the eddic poem Hávamál "Sayings of the High One." In this aggregate of different kinds of verse, Óðinn is the speaker throughout. The myth of the self-sacrifice proper occupies st. 138–41, although much of the rest of the poem seems further concerned with what Óðinn acquired.

"I know that I hung on a windswept tree
nine long nights,
wounded with a spear, dedicated to Odin,
myself to myself,
on that tree of which no man knows
from where its roots run.

With no bread did they refresh me nor a drink from a horn,
downwards I peered;
I took up the runes, screaming I took them,
then I fell back from there.

Nine mighty spells I learnt from the famous son
of Bolthor, Bestla's father,
and I got a drink of the precious mead,
I, soaked from Odrerir.

Then I began to quicken and be wise,
and to grow and to prosper;
one word from another word found a word for me,
one deed from another deed found a deed for me." [*Hávamál*
    st. 138–41]

The windy tree is almost certainly Yggdrasill, the world tree at the center of the cosmos; its name, if it means "Óðinn's steed," would be a reference to this myth. It will be recalled that the spear, Gungnir, was one of Óðinn's attributes; and in *Ynglinga saga* ch. 9 we read about the death of Óðinn, presented here as a prehistoric human king but still with a great many of his mythic attributes:

But when he felt death approaching he had himself marked with the point of a spear, and he declared as his own all men who fell in battle. He said he was about to depart to the abode of the gods and would there welcome his friends. [Hollander 1964: 13]

So death by spear is in theory death in battle, and dead warriors can hope to be welcomed by Óðinn in the abode of the gods. That abode is *Valhǫll*, a transparent compound meaning "carrion hall." Those who join Óðinn there are called *einherjar*, which could mean "those who fight in the same army" or "those who fight as one." Accounts of this place tell of the *einherjar* battling by day and feasting by night.

Writing c. 1070, Adam of Bremen described sacrifices, including human sacrifices, in Uppsala. The bodies were hung in a tree near the temple. Óðinn's self-sacrifice, therefore, invoked the ritual semantics of the god himself and of human sacrifice in pre-Christian times. Consistent with both ritual practice and with the Óðinn mythology, Óðinn takes no food or drink (the same is the case for his vision in *Grímnismál*, except for a drink that seems to enable the ecstatic performance). We cannot be certain whether the myth in *Hávamál* implies a symbolic or actual death and rebirth for Óðinn, but from the perspective of ritual theory that question is irrelevant. What matters is that he went through the ritual and obtained new knowledge. The first sphere of knowledge is runes, which Óðinn takes up screaming, perhaps in agony. Runes were characters in a writing system that originated early in our era, probably based on the Latin alphabet. While there was nothing inherently occult or magic about that writing system, it could be used for such purposes, and that is clearly what the poet has in mind. Indeed, by the time of the Viking Age, a major use of runes was on stones memorializing the recent dead, and that usage too would fit with Óðinn's connection with death and the dead.

St. 140 is particularly interesting. Óðinn learned magic songs from his maternal uncle (elsewhere his name is given as Bǫlþorn), that is, from a giant, indicating that the giants could be sources of wisdom. Given that Óðinn had killed a close male relative of Bǫlþor(n), the dynamics of that exchange are intriguing, and in thinking about it one must weigh the relationship of maternal uncle against the mythological fact that virtually everything the gods get from the giants they take by force or steal. We have already looked at Snorri's version of the acquisition of the mead of poetry. This stanza may simply allude to it, or it may represent an alternative version, although it is always possible that the self-sacrifice enabled the theft of the mead from Suttungr or even that while his body was on the tree, Óðinn embarked on a soul-journey. Snorri wrote in *Ynglinga saga* ch. 7:

> Óthin could shift his appearance. When he did so his body would lie there as if he were asleep or dead; but he himself, in an instant, in the shape of a bird or animal, a fish or a serpent, went to distant countries on his or other men's errands. [Hollander 1964: 10]

This clearly represents a description of a shamanic séance. The role of shamanism in the pre-Christian religion of the North has been the subject of a lively scholarly discussion, and there must be some connection between *seiðr* and shamanism, but other than this passage from *Ynglinga saga* there is little to connect the mythology with shamanism.

Besides myths of acquisition, we may talk of myths of giant-slaying and myths of verbal duels. Þórr is deeply wrapped up with the first and Óðinn with the second.

The *dróttkvætt* poem *Þórsdrápa* "Þórr's *drápa*" (a *drápa* was a structurally formal poem equipped with a refrain) was composed by Eilífr Goðrúnarson in the court of Hákon Sigurðarson, the jarl (the word is cognate with English *earl* but means something more like "major chieftain") of Lade in present-day Trondheim in western Norway near the very end of the tenth century. It is an account of a journey undertaken by Þórr to the abode of a giant, Geirrøðr (not to be confused with the human king Geirrøðr in *Grímnismál*); Snorri too has a version in *Skáldskaparmál*. Both versions indicate that Loki instigated the journey, but only *Skáldskaparmál* spells it out: Loki was captured and starved by the giant and only released when he promised to send Þórr to the giant unarmed with his hammer or gloves of strength. The two versions differ in that Þjálfi, a human, accompanies Þórr in Eilífr's poem, whereas Loki accompanies Þórr in Snorri's version.

Snorri explains in *Gylfaginning* how Þjálfi became Þórr's servant. Loki and Þórr were traveling when they stayed one night with a certain farmer and his family. Þórr slaughtered and cooked the goats who pull his chariot and ordered the family as they ate to throw the bones onto the goatskins. The next morning Þórr revived the goats with his hammer, and one was lame because Þjálfi had broken a ham-bone to get at the marrow. Þórr went into a terrifying rage but calmed down when he saw the fear of the humans and accepted as compensation the service of Þjálfi and his sister Rǫskva (who plays no further role in the mythology as we know it today). The close relationship between Þórr and Þjálfi is not replicated for other gods in the mythology and may indicate that within the religion Þórr was more approachable for humans.

On the way to Geirrøðr, Þórr and his companion must cross a perilous river. Snorri quotes a stanza in an eddic meter, suggesting that this myth was conveyed in a now lost eddic poem too, ordering the river not to rise up. He then sees that a giantess is at fault.

> Then Thor saw up in a certain cleft that Geirrod's daughter Gialp was standing astride the river and she was causing it to rise. Then Thor took up out of the river a great stone and threw it at her and said:
>
> "At its outlet must a river be stemmed."
>
> He did not miss what he was aiming at.... [Faulkes 1987: 82]

Whether the issue was urine or menstrual fluid, Þórr was not finished with female giants. When he reached Geirrøðr's abode he stayed in a goat shed and sat on a chair that began to rise threateningly toward the ceiling. Þórr pushed back and heard a crack and screams: Gjálp and her sister Greip were under the chair pushing it up, and he had broken their backs.

Þórr then proceeded to an encounter with the giantesses' father, Geirrøðr. Geirrøðr threw a lump of molten iron at Þórr, who caught it (with his iron gloves, according to Snorri). Þórr then threw it back and killed the giant with it (Snorri says that the giant ducked behind a pillar and that Þórr threw it through both the pillar and the giant and the wall behind him). This myth must have been widely known, since Saxo Grammaticus has a version of it in *Gesta Danorum*, and a late rather comic tale, *Þorsteins þáttr bœjarmagns* "The Tale of Þorsteinn Strong-as-a house," seems to draw on its plot. Beyond that, there is an episode in some kings' sagas about King Haraldr harðráði (hard-rule) and one of his skalds, Þjóðólfr Árnórsson, who overhear a quarrel between a tanner and an ironsmith. The king challenges Þjóðólfr to compose a *dróttkvætt* stanza about the quarrel making of one of them Þórr and the other Geirrøðr, a task Þjóðólfr accomplishes with apparent ease.

Another important giant-slaying myth concerns Þórr's duel with Hrungnir. It is told both in Snorri's *Skáldskaparmál* and in Þjóðólfr's *Haustlǫng*, mentioned earlier as a source of the myth of the reacquisition of Iðunn and her apples; the shield Þjóðólfr is describing was thus decorated with scenes from more than one myth. Þjóðólfr's account begins with Þórr's journey to Hrungnir, which is portentous: the skies are burning, hail batters the earth, which is splitting asunder while rocks shake and crags burst apart (st. 15–16; perhaps an earthquake or volcanic eruption?). Because it was the will of the gods and *dísir*, Hrungnir stood on his shield (st. 17) and Þórr killed him (st. 18). The giant's whetstone flew toward Þórr and lodged in his forehead (st. 19) until a woman could enchant it out (st. 20).

This is a case where Snorri's version, also in *Skáldskaparmál*, differs significantly from the older poetic source. Snorri motivates the story as follows. Óðinn is out riding and gets in a dispute with the giant Hrungnir about the quality of their horses; Hrungnir rides furiously after Óðinn and when the two end up in Ásgarðr, Óðinn offers him hospitality. Quickly drunk, the giant boasts that he will take with him Valhǫll, bury Ásgarðr, and kill all the gods except

Freyja and Sif, whom he will take with him as well. The gods invoke Þórr, who is enraged at the sight of a giant making drunken boasts while Freyja is serving him ale, but the giant says that he is under Óðinn's protection and, furthermore, is unarmed:

> "And it has been a very foolish thing for me to do," he said, "to leave behind at home my shield and whetstone, but if I had my weapons here, we would hold the duel now, but as it is I declare you will be guilty of baseness if you go and kill me when I am unarmed." [Faulkes 1987: 78]

With "baseness" Hrungnir invokes the hyper-masculine code of honor, but Þórr is eager for a formal duel anyway, since he has never before engaged in one. Everyone understands that the outcome will be highly significant, for Hrungnir is the strongest of giants.

Now Snorri has Þórr make his cosmic journey, but he has Þjálfi with him. This is no doubt because a duel, as we know from various accounts, required a second who was to hold the dueler's shield for him. The giant's second is a clay monster of enormous proportions but with the heart of a mare, which cultural knowledge told the audience was a clear sign that he was a coward. When the duel commenced, Þjálfi warned the giant that Þórr would attack from underground, thus tricking the giant into standing on his shield. God and giant hurled their weapons at the same time, and the hammer and whetstone met in mid-air. The hammer went on to kill the giant, and a portion of the whetstone was lodged in Þórr's head. The giant fell over Þórr, his leg pinning Þórr to the ground. His son Magni (a noun meaning "might"), a precocious three-year-old (three *days* old in some manuscripts) lifts the leg to free his father. The sorceress Gróa chants the whetstone most of the way out of Þórr's head but is distracted when Þórr, thinking to reward her, tells her that he carried her father Aurvandill from Giantlands in a basket. Aurvandill's toe was sticking out of the basket and froze. Þórr threw it up into the sky where it became a star, but the rest of him will be home soon. Her distraction means that according to Snorri the whetstone stays in Þórr's head—not a motif that we see elsewhere.

Because it includes a formal duel, this version of the myth is more than a simple giant-slaying. It also shows us something of the relationship between Óðinn and Þórr: Þórr cleans up a mess that Óðinn made, but a second-generation god is needed to finish the job, and in passing we learn that Þórr was also involved in cosmogony by placing a star in the sky.

Þórr's most famous battle with a giant was his fishing up of the World Serpent, which will be taken up in the following chapter.

Just as Þórr fought giants with his hammer, so Óðinn fought them with his wisdom. One of the myths of verbal duels in which he figures is also a myth of giant-slaying. It is recounted in the eddic poem *Vafþrúðnismál*. In the early stanzas, Óðinn expresses his desire to "contend in ancient matters with that all-wise giant" (st. 1), and Frigg mildly tries to dissuade him, as she knows "no giant to be as powerful as Vafthrudnir is" (st. 2). Óðinn sets off anyway, and when he enters Vafþrúðnir's hall the giant says: "May you not come out of our halls alive / unless you should be the wiser one" (st. 7), a rather overt threat. Identifying himself as Gagnráðr (literally "gain-counsel"), Óðinn easily answers the set of four questions put by Vafþrúðnir, which are essentially cosmological: what are the names of the horses that pull the sun and the moon, the river that separates the giants from the gods, and the battlefield where the final battle will take place. The giant now announces that the loser of the contest will forfeit his life (st. 19), and it is Óðinn's turn to put questions. First he puts twelve questions with the opening formula running from: "Tell me this one thing" to "Tell me this twelfth thing." These questions are essentially cosmogonic, and we have seen some of them earlier: what were the origin of the earth, moon, sun, seasons, the wind, and the race of giants; how did they procreate; how did Njǫrðr come to join the gods; who are the *einherjar*; but finally, how do you know so much? To this last question the giant responds that he has traveled through all the worlds. Óðinn now puts a final set of six questions, each of which begins with the impressive statement "Much have I traveled, / much have I tried out, / much have I tested the Powers." The first four focus on the aftermath of Ragnarøk: how will the sun be replaced, and what beings will survive? The fifth focuses on Óðinn's own fate at Ragnarøk, and this too the giant knows. But the sixth is: "What did Odin say into his son's ear / before he mounted the pyre?" This question about Baldr's funeral undoes Vafþrúðnir:

> "No man knows what you said in bygone days
> into your son's ear;
> with doomed mouth I've spoken my ancient lore
> about the fate of the gods;
> I've been contending with Odin in words of wisdom;
> you'll always be the wisest of beings." [*Vafþrúðnismál* st. 55]

Although it is nowhere stated explicitly, we are justified in inferring that just as Hrungnir was the strongest of giants, Vafþrúðnir was the wisest. The physical and verbal duels very clearly order the gods above the giants in the hierarchy of beings. *Grímnismál*, already mentioned several times, is not technically a verbal duel, since Óðinn is the only speaker, but like *Vafþrúðnismál* it traffics in wisdom, and Óðinn's identity is revealed to the human king Geirrøðr at the end; the king rushes to have Óðinn released but stumbles and falls upon his sword, thus dying like Vafþrúðnir. In this case, however, there is an issue of dynastic succession, for Geirrøðr's son, who is also present, will succeed him.

An unlikely verbal duel once took place between Óðinn and Þórr; the source is the eddic poem *Hárbarðsljóð* "Harbard's Song." Þórr wishes to cross an inlet and accosts the ferryman with his ship on the other side, who calls himself *Hárbarðr* "hoary-beard" but is actually Óðinn in disguise. He refuses to ferry Þórr but asks him repeatedly what he has been doing, to which Þórr responds with boasts about his giant-slaying. When Þórr asks Hárbarðr what he has been up to, the responses are elliptical references to magic, seduction, and warfare. Óðinn gets the last word ("Go where the monsters'll get you" [st. 60]), and Þórr does not get the ride; and despite having much to boast about, he clearly loses the verbal duel. In that sense, the poem orders Óðinn hierarchically about Þórr, and Óðinn even taunts Þórr with this perhaps exaggerated claim: "Odin owns the nobles who fall in battle/and Thor owns the race of thralls" (st. 24).

Another eddic poem, *Alvíssmál* "All-wise's Sayings," has Þórr win a verbal duel. Alvíss/All-wise is a dwarf to whom Þórr's daughter was somehow promised in marriage while Þórr was away. Upon learning of this fact, Þórr asks Alvíss for the terms for certain semantic categories in the various worlds, those of gods, humans, giants, the dead, and so forth, and the dwarf's wisdom easily enables him to answer. It does not, however, keep him from realizing that day is about to break, and he is caught by the sun, presumably turning him to stone or causing him to burst.

Finally, I will class as a verbal duel a complex myth about the journey of Þórr, Loki, and Þjálfi to the court of the giant Útgarðaloki, literally "Loki of the Útgarðar (outer enclosures)." On their way they take shelter in a "house" that turns out to be the glove of a literal giant, with whom they agree to travel. The huge man puts all the food into his bag, and at the end of the day tells Þórr and the others to help themselves while he dozes off. Þórr cannot undo the straps and in a rage bashes the sleeping behemoth, who wonders whether a leaf just fell on him. Twice more Þórr bashes him, with similar results. In the morning they part ways and the divine team come to Útgarðaloki's courts. There they are asked to participate in games, where their showing is miserable. Þjálfi runs a footrace with Hugi, which he loses. Loki has an eating contest with Logi, which he loses. Þórr is charged with draining a drinking horn, lifting a cat, and wrestling an old woman, Elli, and cannot quite complete the tasks. When it is time for the humiliated guests to leave, Útgarðaloki escorts them out and explains it all. He himself had "deceived you by appearances" (Faulkes 1987: 44–45) as the gigantic traveling companion. He had fastened the food sack with trip wire, and he had moved a nearby mountain under Þórr's hammer blows, which had caused three valleys to form. It is in what happened in the contests that we move into the realm of the verbal, for *hugi* is the simple noun for thought, *logi* for fire, and *elli* for old age. The drinking horns were attached to the ocean, and in trying to drain them Þórr caused tides to come into being. The cat was actually the World Serpent, and it was a prodigious feat to be able to move it even a little bit. The message is therefore somewhat mixed: Þórr and his companions failed to see that a noun could be its referent, and they could be deceived by trickery, but Þórr's actions were to some degree cosmogonic.

These myths of (re)acquisition, giant-slaying, and verbal dueling show that although the gods have a margin over the giants, it is slim. The very fact that Þórr struggles with old age suggests the mortality of the gods, and that is the point of the myths of Baldr's death and Ragnarøk.

We have parts of the myth of Baldr's death in *dróttkvætt* poetry, eddic poems, Snorri's *Gylfaginning*, and Saxo's *Gesta Danorum*. Naturally the versions differ considerably, and it is a mistake to try to reconstruct a single proper form. Nevertheless, much is constant, and the versions are for the most part consistent with a common core: Óðinn's son Baldr was fated to die; his brother Hǫðr killed him; another brother Váli, sired by Óðinn for the purpose, avenged him; Baldr was celebrated in a funeral; the death was portentous.

Eddic poems add a few additional details to this skeleton. According to *Vǫluspá* st. 31–32 (found in only one of the two main manuscripts), the weapon that killed Baldr was a dart made from mistletoe. In *Lokasenna* st. 28, Loki tells Frigg, "I brought it about that you will never again/see Baldr ride to the halls." *Vǫluspá* st. 34–35 suggest that vengeance was also taken on Loki for the death of Baldr.

Baldr's funeral is described in a late tenth-century Icelandic *dróttkvætt* poem by Úlfr Uggason, *Húsdrápa* "House-poem." The title refers to the fact that the poem describes carvings in the wainscoting in a newly built hall that was to be used for a wedding. The stanzas relating to the funeral consist first of a description of a procession

FIGURE 1.5 One of the tapestries from the Oseberg ship funeral, dated to the early ninth century (Kulturhistorisk museum, Oslo no. C 55000_337_1 and C 55000_337_2). Drawing by Mary Storm. Photo: Mårten Teigen, Kulturhistorisk museum, Universitetet i Oslo, Oslo.

of gods (Freyr, Heimdallr, Óðinn) riding to the funeral, along with valkyries and ravens, symbols of death.[8] A tapestry from the ship burial at Oseberg, Norway, appears to show a procession, in context probably a funeral procession [figure 1.5], which suggests that human funerals may to some degree have reflected Baldr's funeral in the world of the gods.

After the procession comes this puzzling half-stanza:

The exceedingly strong Hildr <valkyrie> of the mountains [GI-ANTESS] made the sea-Sleipnir <horse> [SHIP] lumber forward, and the companions of Hroptr <=Óðinn> killed the steed with helmet-fires. [SWORDS] [Marold et al. 2017: 422]

---

[8] As is often the case, the stanzas of this poem are not found in sequence but are scattered in Snorri's *Skáldskaparmál*, where they are used to exemplify various kennings. Editors must reconstruct the order. In this case, the word "first" occurs with Freyr, so he leads the procession, and after the lines about Valkyries and ravens there is a refrain, which usually signals the end of a section of a poem. Although editors used to put the Óðinn stanza before the Heimdallr stanza, the latest editors, Edith Marold et al. (2017), reverse that order.

Snorri explains some of these strange details in *Gylfaginning* and adds a new dimension concerning the permanence of Baldr's death. Baldr was having bad dreams suggesting that his life was in danger, and in response the gods decided to get oaths from all kinds of danger not to harm him. His mother Frigg obtained these promises, and thenceforth the gods amused themselves by flinging weapons and stones at Baldr, all of which fell harmlessly to the ground. "But when Loki Laufeyjarson saw this he was not pleased that Baldr was unharmed" (Faulkes 1987: 48). In the form of an old woman he quizzed Frigg about the oath-taking and learned that she had exempted mistletoe. He brought some mistletoe to the assembly and directed the hand of Baldr's blind brother Hǫðr to throw it. It penetrated Baldr and that was his death. Frigg, however, sought and obtained a volunteer to go to visit the world of the dead and see whether Hel would release Baldr. Hermóðr volunteered and set off on Sleipnir. Hel promised to release Baldr if everything would weep for him, but one old woman in a cave, calling herself Þǫkk "Thanks," refused, reciting this verse:

"Thanks will weep dry tears for Baldr's burial. No good got I from the old one's son either dead or alive. Let Hel hold what she has. [Faulkes 1987: 51]

Snorri goes on to say that people assume that the old woman was actually Loki.

Snorri adds some details to the funeral, of which the most important is perhaps that the funeral ship could not be launched until Óðinn summoned a giantess, presumably the subject of st. 11 of *Húsdrápa* just cited, who shoved the ship down the rollers. She had arrived riding a wolf with snakes for reins (perhaps reflected in an image on a southern Swedish picture stone; see figure 1.6), and Óðinn's men were unable to look after it without knocking it down.

Many scholars read st. 11 thus. The translation of Marold et al. is based on the idea that a horse-sacrifice may have taken place at the funeral. There is no compelling reason to accept one reading or the other.

FIGURE 1.6 Female figure riding a wolf on a picture stone from Hunnestad in Skåne, Sweden (DR 284, Samnordisk runtextdatabas), perhaps Hyrrokkin riding on a wolf to Baldr's funeral. Photo: Roberto Fortuna, Nationalmuseet, København.

Unlike the eddic poems, Snorri does not tell about vengeance taken on Hǫðr by Váli, whom Óðinn sires on a giantess. Rather he has all the vengeance directed at Loki, who is bound under a poisonous snake, where he will stay until Ragnarøk.

The version in Saxo is quite different, since although Balderus (= Baldr) is a demi-god, his nemesis Høtherus (= Hǫðr) is a human king, and they lead armies against each other, striving for the Danish throne, before Høtherus finally kills Balderus in battle. Saxo does, however, have the siring of the avenger by Othinus (= Óðinn), in this case on a Russian princess, Rinda. He must finally bind and rape her, which is probably parallel to a line in a tenth-century *dróttkvætt* poem stating that Óðinn used *seiðr* on Rindr, the mother of Váli in the Icelandic tradition.

How the various versions of the myth may have been understood in Viking Age or medieval Scandinavia is open to dispute, but the killing within Óðinn's family probably resonated: when one brother kills another in a "self-help" society, the mechanisms of bloodfeud are defeated. Óðinn sires an avenger, but vengeance is taken on Hǫðr, who is, just like Baldr, an offspring of Óðinn. Typologically, Snorri's version of the failed attempt to retrieve Baldr from the world of the dead parallels myths from around the world that explain the origin of death and/or its irreversibility. But it also puts the blame squarely on Loki, originally a giant, and Óðinn's blood-brother. Each had presumably sworn to avenge the other, but that is moot now. Loki has contrived to bring death to the gods, and a killing within their family may reflect the original killing within a family, that of Ymir. Once one god can die at the hands of the giants, they all can. Thus the death of Baldr ushers in Ragnarøk.

The first component of this compound, *ragna-*, is genitive of the neuter plural noun *regin* "(divine) powers." The second component occurs in various forms;[9] the common sense is "judgment" although another form means "twilight." The two can perhaps be reconciled if we take them both to mean "end," and anyone familiar with the mythology would know that *ragnarøk*, which is referred to fairly often, meant the end of the world, in that gods and giants would kill each other and the cosmos would be destroyed.

---

[9] I follow the argument put forth by Haraldur Bernharðsson (2007), based on orthographic evidence, that the earliest form of the second component was *røk*. However, I find his suggestion that the original meaning in this particular context might have been "rebirth" difficult to follow.

In the version of *Vǫluspá* in the *Poetic Edda*, the seeress recounts a series of disquieting visions after telling of Baldr's death, the vengeance on Hǫðr, and the binding of Loki. St. 39 (st. 38 in Larrington's translation) is particularly chilling:

> There she saw wading in turbid streams
> false-oath swearers and murderers,
> and the seducer of another man's close confidante;
> there Nidhogg sucks the corpses of the dead—
> a wolf tears at men—do you want to know more: and what?

The gods themselves have been oath-breakers, murderers, and seducers, and so it seems that their (mis)behavior has now spread to the entire world. We have already seen Níðhǫggr, rending the world ash Yggdrasill from below, and st. 66 (st. 62 in Larrington's translation) at the end of the poem tells us that it is a flying dragon, a gleaming snake. Its actions, and those of the wolf, mean that the dead do not rest in peace as they should, thus rendering death ritual useless.

St. 45 (st. 44 in Larrington's translation) highlights the social breakdowns that occur as the cosmos is threatened:

> Brother will fight brother and be his slayer,
> sister's sons will violate the kinship-bond;
> hard it is in the world, whoredom abounds,
> axe-age, sword-age, shields are cleft asunder,
> wind-age, wolf-age, before the world plunges headlong;
> no man will spare another.

The bonds of kinship dissolve as battle erupts, and the world "plunges headlong." Again I would point out that brothers have already killed brothers (Hǫðr and Váli). A literal translation of the following line ("sister's sons will violate the kinship-bond") would be: "cousins will destroy affinal kinship," which has already happened when the gods kill giants. Thus the seeds of the end were planted in the beginning.

Vǫluspá and the other sources see the end as a battle with a series of individual combats, in which gods and giants kill each other.

Despite vengeance taken on Fenrir, the wolf who kills Óðinn, by another of his sons, Víðarr (see figure 1.7), the demise of the cosmos the gods had created now follows. The ordering of the heavenly

FIGURE 1.7 The rune stone at Ledberg in Östergötland (Ög 181, Samnordisk runtextdatabas). According to Snorri in *Gylfaginning*, Víðarr avenged his father Óðinn, whom the wolf Fenrir had slain, by placing one foot in the lower jaw of the wolf and grasping its upper jaw to tear apart its mouth (Faulkes 1987: 54). Photo: Cecilia Ljung.

bodies is undone as the earth sinks into a fiery sea (in myth this is not contradictory).

> The sun turns black, land sinks into the sea,
> the bright stars vanish from the sky;
> steam rises up in the conflagration,
> hot flame plays high against heaven itself. [*Vǫluspá* st. 57; st.
> 54 in Larrington]

And yet the gods and cosmos have a future after all. The earth rises anew from the sea, and it is peopled with the sons of the old gods. These include Hǫðr and Baldr, who are reconciled in this new world in a way that was impossible in the old, and also a daughter of the sun. Two human beings survive to populate the earth. This new cosmos was not the result of a killing within a family, so maybe it has a chance to survive. The Hauksbók version of *Vǫluspá* links the new cosmos fairly unambiguously to Christianity:

> Then comes the mighty one
> to the judgment of the Powers,
> full of strength, from above,
> he who rules over all. [*Vǫluspá, Hauksbók text* st. 59]

But the final stanza in both full versions offers a vision of Níðhǫggr, just before the seeress announces, in the third person, that she will sink down into the earth, whence she came:

> There comes the shadow-dark dragon flying,
> the gleaming serpent, up from Dark-of-moon Hills;
> Nidhogg flies over the plain, in his pinions he carries
> corpses; now she will sink down. [*Vǫluspá* st. 66; Larrington 62]

We know that notions of Ragnarøk were powerful, since we have allusions to it in a number of poems from the tenth century. At least two of these make it clear that Óðinn is gathering troops, the *einherjar*, for the last battle (see Resources later in this book). A line from the poem *Eiríksmál*, usually dated to just after the battle of Stainmore (Northumbria) was fought, where Eiríkr blóðøx fell in 954, has Óðinn say that: "the grey wolf is gazing at the abodes of the gods."

This chapter has organized the mythology into a linear sequence, and that sequence is certainly to be glimpsed in *Vǫluspá* and in Snorri's *Gylfaginning*. The myths of acquisition and reacquisition, of giant-slaying, and of verbal dueling would be understood within this sequence as occurring during the "mythic present," as I termed it earlier—that is, after the creation of the cosmos and before its demise and rebirth. We should, however, be wary of creating a system that is too neat. Not only was there no requirement of the oral mythology to be consistent, there was, as I mentioned in the Introduction, no way to check for consistency, no canonical text to appeal to. We must understand, too, that the corpus of Old Norse mythology is quite restricted compared to other oral mythologies, and if we had more texts we would probably have more inconsistences. When we have even just a few versions, as in the myth of Þórr's fishing expedition, which we will take up in the next chapter, we see significant inconsistencies.

Chapter 2

Old Norse Mythology as Sacred Narrative

Þórr's Fishing Expedition

This chapter comprises a case study of what was probably the most widely known myth of the most widely venerated god in the Viking Age North, namely Þórr's fishing up of the World Serpent.[1] We will look first at the texts that have survived from pre-Christian Scandinavia, namely *dróttkvætt* poetry, before turning to the more accessible sources, namely the central section of the eddic poem *Hymiskviða* and Snorri's rather complete version in *Gylfaginning*; the claims of these last two texts to the status of "sacred narrative" are fraught, as was discussed in the Introduction. By the same token, the far-flung rock carvings, which almost certainly do date to the pre-Christian period, deserve close attention. Although the myth must be read against the pattern of giant-slaying myths set forth in the preceding chapter, Þórr does not kill the serpent in all versions of the myth that are left to us, and that variation complicates interpretation considerably.

---

[1] For a stimulating alternative presentation of the same case study, see Abram (2011: 31–50).

Background

Þórr's encounter with the World Serpent (one of Loki's monstrous offspring and also known as Jǫrmungandr) has left more traces from the pre-Christian and medieval North than any other aspect of the mythology. We have two *dróttkvætt* sequences whose pre-Christian provenance has not been seriously challenged. One is from Bragi Boddason inn gamli "the old," the first attested skald, who was probably Norwegian and active perhaps as early as the later ninth century, and the other formed part of the *Húsdrápa* of Úlfr Uggason, from late tenth-century western Iceland. There are also numerous *dróttkvætt* fragments. Given the existence of Viking Age rock carvings of the encounter between Þórr and the serpent, making a swath from Sweden to Northumbria, it is plain that the subject was one that had visual appeal. Alongside these two *dróttkvætt* poems and some shorter *dróttkvætt* fragments are the eddic poem *Hymiskviða* and Snorri's narrative in *Gylfaginning*. These both put the narrative in Iceland in the thirteenth century, although *Hymiskviða* must in my view have an extensive oral prehistory. Certainly I find it likely that versions of the story of Þórr's encounter with the monster must have existed in oral poetry of the eddic (common Germanic) sort in many times and places. The Indo-European analogues, such as the encounters between Indra and Vrtra, or Apollo and Python (see, e.g., Schröder 1955), suggest that some form of the story may have existed even before the period of Germanic migration, and if so there is no reason to imagine that it did not exist in verse form—the form that was later to be used in Old English, Old High German, Old Saxon, and of course in the North, in eddic poetry and on some runic inscriptions (see Introduction).

In *Skáldskaparmál*, Snorri wrote this:

> How shall Loki be referred to? By calling him son of Farbauti and Laufey, of Nal, brother of Byleist and Helblindi, father of Vanargand, i.e. Fenriswolf, and of Iormundgand, i.e. the Midgard serpent .... [Faulkes 1987: 76]

This passage certifies Loki as the father of the World Serpent and also assigns the name Jǫrmungandr to the beast. The first component of Jǫrmungandr is clearly the intensifier *jǫrmun-* "power-." The second component is usually construed as "stick" or "staff," and if this construction is correct, we can compare the image of the straight stick Jǫrmungandr with the image of the curve or circle around the earth implied by the name Miðgarðsormr and captured in such kennings as "necklace of the earth." It is worth noting, however, that *gandr* can also mean "wolf," and "power-wolf" could perhaps be a plausible designation for the World Serpent.

Snorri explains the birth and fate of these "sticks" or "wolves" in a famous passage in *Gylfaginning*, discussed in the previous chapter, explaining the binding of Fenrisúlfr. Alongside this elaborate story are brief notices to the effect that the World Serpent was cast into the sea and Hel into the underworld. Snorri's words in *Gylfaginning* about the World Serpent paint a remarkable picture:

> And when they came to him he threw the serpent into that deep sea which lies round all lands, and this serpent grew so that it lies in the midst of the ocean encircling all lands and bites on its own tail. [Faulkes 1987: 27]

Snorri presumably had in mind here a medieval map (presumably a so-called T-O map, as in figure 2.1), and the deep sea is at the outer edges around all the lands, settled and unsettled. In biting its own tail, the World Serpent forms a gripping beast typical of the animal ornamentation of Viking Age art (see figure 2.2), but whether there is any relationship between the mythic image recorded by Snorri and the visual image of Viking Age art must remain unknown. If there is, it is not inconceivable that Snorri is accommodating the World Serpent to art he had seen. While many, from Jung to the Theosophists, have seen the *ouroboros* as a universal symbol, what Snorri probably had in mind with the tail-biting was closing off any gap or way around the beast for sailors

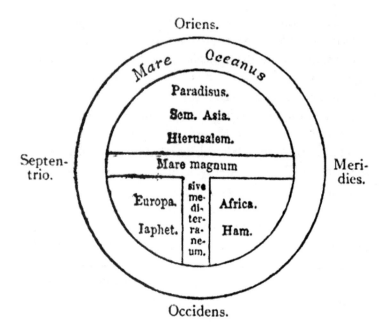

Oriens.

Mare Oceanus

Paradisus.

Sem. Asia.

Hierusalem.

Septen-
trio.

Mare magnum

sive
me-
di-
ter-
ra-
ne-
um.

Europa.

Africa.

Iaphet.

Ham.

Meri-
dies.

Occidens.

FIGURE 2.1 T-O schematic map from Isidore of Seville's *Origines*, France, twelfth century. Photo: Wikimedia Commons, from *Encyclopedia Brittanica*, 11th ed. The map is oriented (literally) with east (*oriens*) on top, thus properly placing Europe to the north (bottom left) and Africa to the south (bottom right). Around the three continents is *mare oceanum* (the Ocean sea).

at sea. Surely this notion contributed to the choice of Þórr as the god on whom Helgi the lean, otherwise a Christian convert, called when at sea.[2]

Situated as he is in the deep sea, far from human habitation, the World Serpent is rather like an outlaw, in the wilds and beyond the

[2] This information is found in a version of *Landnámabók* "Book of settlements," an early Icelandic history of the settling of the island. Helgi was supposedly the original settler of Eyjafjörður in the north of Iceland. *Landnámabók* (ch. S208/H184) reports that he was "much mixed in faith; he believed in Christ but called on Þórr for sea voyages and difficult situations," and that when he first sighted Iceland from the sea he called upon Þórr to help him determine exactly where to settle.

FIGURE 2.2 Viking Age bronze and tortoise-shell brooch with "gripping beasts," from the Ashmoleon Museum's collection, c. 8th–11th century. Photo: HIP/Art Resource, NY.

legal constraints that bind men's actions. It is for this reason that Þórr can attack and possibly kill the beast, even though it is the son of Loki, who is also numbered among the Æsir. Even if that is so, the Icelandic sagas teach us that relatives of slain outlaws still thirst for vengeance.

Let us turn now to the texts themselves. First we will examine the skalds whose verse about this myth has survived.

Bragi Boddason

The first skald is usually understood to have been Bragi Boddason, who was active in Norway in the ninth century. Six half-stanzas survive that are attributed to him and describe this myth. They are, therefore, the oldest textual evidence, and as I stated in the Introduction, it is likely that surviving stanzas ascribed to the skalds give us a fairly accurate picture of what some of the underlying oral texts sounded like during the pre-Christian period—in other words, when these texts constituted sacred narrative. Here, however, we must mention a conundrum. To Bragi is ascribed a shield-poem, *Ragnarsdrápa* "Ragnar's (formal) poem," that is, a poem based on images incised into a shield. Some editors think that the half-stanzas about the fishing expedition constitute a part of that poem, while others do not, including the most recent editor, Margaret Clunies Ross. If they do not constitute an ekphrasis of a shield, as Clunies Ross believes, the six half-stanzas would have a more direct claim to sacred narrative than if they comprise an ekphrasis; they would be from a poem about or more likely directed to the god. It should also be noted that, once again, the half-stanzas are not found consecutively, but are rather cited individually in Snorri's *Skáldskaparmál*. The order is thus up to the editor, but a chronological arrangement like the one taken by Clunies Ross and titled as "Þórr's Fishing" seems reasonable.[3]

1   It is conveyed to me that the son of mankind's father [=Óðinn > =Þórr] soon wanted to try his strength against the twisted thing of the earth [=Miðgarðsormr], pounded by water.

2   The fishing line of Viðrir's <=Óðinn's> heir [=Þórr] lay not at all slack on the ski of Eynæfir <sea-king> [SHIP], when

---

[3] For the conventions used in the translations of *dróttkvætt* poetry, see the Preface.

Jǫrmungandr <=Miðgarðsormr> unwound himself on the sand.

3 The terrifier of Ǫflugbarði <giant> [=Þórr] lifted the hammer in his right hand, when he recognized the boundary-saithe of all lands [=Miðgarðsormr].[4]

4 And the ugly ring of the road of the side-rowed ship [SEA > =Miðgarðsormr] glared from below, defiant, at the skull-splitter of Hrungnir <giant> [=Þórr].

5 When the coiling eel of the drink of the Vǫlsungar [POISON > =Miðgarðsormr] hung coiled up on the fishing hook of the wrestling-challenger of the followers of ancient Litr <giant> [GIANTS > =Þórr].

6 The wind-sender of the sea [giant = Hymir] did not want to raise up the twisted terrifier, he who cut the slender string of the marshland of seagulls [SEA > FISHING LINE] for Þórr. [Clunies Ross 2017a: 46–53]

The verb "conveyed" (literally "sent") in st. 1 implies the physical conveyance of something, presumably perhaps an artifact with an image on it, and some manuscripts have "shown" here instead, suggesting that the poet has seen an image. This, then, is the context in which the poem should probably be understood: Bragi may have before him some physical manifestation of the story. Even so, the narrative information in the first stanza, that Þórr wishes to test himself against the serpent, would have been difficult to express in an image and probably belonged only to the oral tradition. This information sets the story in motion, and it makes sense. It creates a parallel with the encounters that Óðinn seeks out in eddic verse, not least the contest of wisdom with Vafþrúðnir. Indeed, if Þórr's encounter with Hrungnir, the strongest giant, parallels directly that of Óðinn with

---

[4] The fish "saithe" (*Pollachius virens*) is generally known as "pollock" in the United States. However, for the purposes of the kenning, any ocean-fish would do.

Vafþrúðnir, the wisest giant, the encounter with the World Serpent provides a different kind of parallel, namely the seeking out of the opponent and meeting with him in his own territory.

Such travel is how Þórr operates, although he usually goes east: as he boasts in *Hárbarðsljóð* st. 23: "I was in the east, and I fought against giants." This aspect of Þórr's mythological role is so well known that it can simply be alluded to, as in the prose header to *Lokasenna*: "Thor did not come, because he was away in the east." Note, too, that the myth of the duel with Hrungnir began in both accounts, in *Haustlǫng* and *Skáldskaparmál*, with vivid descriptions of the god's travel to the site of the duel, which is clearly somewhere outside the abode of the gods. It is worth pausing to consider the implications of locating Þórr's fights with giants in the wild places where giants lived. Þórr is making the world safe not just in the center but also in the peripheral areas of the cosmos. Giants live for the most part in the mountains and uninhabited areas, and the serpent lives in the sea—probably the deep waters beyond the usual fishing banks, as Snorri explicitly states in his version of this myth (*Gylfaginning*, Faulkes 1987: 47).

From st. 2, the story as it is told here appears to be quite visual, a portrait in words of the moment when Þórr has hooked the monster with his fishing line. The line is taut (st. 2); þórr brandishes his hammer (st. 3); the serpent gazes balefully up from the sea (st. 4) as he is hooked on the line (st. 5). When Þórr recognizes the serpent in st. 3, we must assume that his gaze is focused on the serpent in an analogue to st. 4 (and here we should recall that the original order of the verses is not known, and st. 4 might have preceded st. 3; the effect would be immaterial). St. 6 must come at the end of the sequence, for in it a giant cuts the fishing line.

Dróttkvætt poetry relies at least as much for its effect on its language, especially kennings, as on its narrative per se. The kennings for Þórr begin with family relationship: Bragi portrays him as "son of mankind's father" and "Viðrir's heir" in the first of the two half-stanzas, in both cases, therefore, attaching him to Óðinn. Then follow kennings relying on Þórr as enemy of chaos beings: "terrifier of Ǫflugbarði," "skull-splitter of Hrungnir," and "wrestling-challenger of the followers of ancient Litr." Direct reference to the Hrungnir myth seems particularly appropriate in the context of a cosmic duel, and Litr was the name of a dwarf whom Þórr kicked into the pyre at Baldr's funeral, according to Snorri;[5] Ǫflugbarði ("Mightily bearded one") is otherwise unknown. As we shall see, kennings of family relationship and kennings of monster-slaying typify skalds' presentation of Þórr throughout the corpus of verse about this encounter.

Unlike Þórr, who has a famous father, the serpent is misshapen (a "twisted thing" in st. 1, "twisted" in st. 6—an unrelated noun and adjective are used), an "ugly ring" (st. 4) and a "coiling eel" (st. 5) who has "unwound" himself on the sea-floor (st. 2). The cosmic aspects of the drama are captured in the determinants of the kennings "twisted thing *of the earth*" and especially "boundary-saithe *of all lands*." And if Þórr is the "terrifier of Ǫflugbarði," the serpent is just a "twisted terrifier," or, if one construes the kenning in another way, "twisted terrifier of the water." These kennings capture the meeting between order and disorder that the fishing expedition constitutes.

One final example will show the remarkable interpretive possibilities of this hypersubtle verse form. The giant who cuts the line is the "breeze-sender of the water" (or just the "breeze-sender" if we construe "of the water" as the determinant of "terrifier"). The kenning means giant because, as we learn in *Vafþrúðnismál* st. 37, Hræsvelgr "sits at heaven's end,/a giant in eagle's shape;/from his wings, they say, the wind blows over all men." Hræsvelgr means "corpse-swallower," and it is tempting to associate the name with the usefulness of a brisk wind during a cremation. But Þórr, too, is associated with the wind, as we shall see in the next chapter. So the

---

[5] Scholars have long understood Litr as a giant-name in this passage, since it is parallel to the other giant-names in the adjacent kennings. If it is the dwarf who is referred to here, it is because he too was a victim of Þórr. As his encounter with the dwarf Alvíss suggests, the relationship of Þórr to dwarfs was likely to have been uneasy.

choice of this kenning for the giant who thwarts Þórr's effort to fish up the serpent suggests a contrast or conflict between giant and Þórr. At the moment when the giant cut the line, the poet presents him as an opposing wind-force. We can imagine a storm at sea, with furious winds tearing the tops off the waves as the serpent gazes balefully at Þórr brandishing his hammer.

Bragi also calls the protagonists by their names: Jǫrmungandr (st. 2, unless he intended *jǫrmungandr* as a kenning)[6] and Þórr (st. 6). These direct namings would be particularly apt if an image of the fight were at hand, since the names would, as it were, be "visible" in the figures—that is, the figures would be easy to identify.

Qlvir hnúfa

In the section on how to ken Þórr, *Skáldskaparmál* contains these lines, attributed to Qlvir hnúfa:

> The encircler of all lands [= Miðgarðsormr] and the son of Jǫrð
> <goddess> [= Þórr] became violent. [Clunies Ross 2017f: 491]

Sources tell us that Qlvir was a court poet of Haraldr hárfagri "fairhair" in Norway and that he participated in the battle of Hafrsfjǫrðr c. 872. Since Haraldr ruled until c. 930 we cannot date the verse with any certainty, but it certainly provides evidence of the centrality of the myth among Viking Age poets in Norway.

This fragment merely tells us that the two opponents "became violent." The verb in question is used especially of natural phenomena such as fire and the sea. Thus we may well be justified in taking this brief fragment as an indication of the cosmic nature of

---

[6] The reasoning here would be that "power-stick" would make a possible kenning for the serpent, and that Snorri later took it as a personal name.

the encounter between Þórr and the World Serpent: like roaring flames or crashing sea, they rage at one another. Perhaps it is not going too far to say that a statement to the effect that Þórr and the World Serpent raged at one another (perhaps like fire or the sea) points to the very middle of the encounter, not to its beginning or end. Perhaps Ǫlvir, like Bragi (and the rock carvers, as we shall see), meant to focus on the very moment when Þórr had hooked the serpent.

Úlfr Uggason

Snorri records at various places in *Skáldsksparmál* twelve stanzas (more often half-stanzas, actually) that he attributes to Úlfr Uggason's *Húsdrápa* "House-Poem," mentioned earlier in connection with Baldr's funeral, a poem based on the decorations carved into the wainscoting in a late tenth-century Icelandic hall and thus an ekphrasis.

Because the stanzas are scattered throughout Skáldskaparmál, as with Bragi's stanzas, arranging them is an editorial matter. Here I follow the order adopted by the latest editors, Edith Marold et al.:

3 The interior-moon of the forehead [EYE] of the hostile friend of the gods [= Þórr] shone; the praise-blessed god shot terror-beams at the necklace of the earth [= Miðgarðsormr].

4 And the flashing-eyed stiff cord of the earth [= Miðgarðsormr] stared at the tester of the peoples of the bone of the earth [ROCK > GIANTS > = Þórr] below the ship's side and blew poison.

5 The user of goats [= Þórr] said that it seemed a very great danger to the heavy-set fat one from the weighty powerful pull.

6 The most powerful killer of the mountain-Gautr <man of the Gautar> [GIANT > = Þórr] let his fist slam against the ear of

the tester of the bone of the reed [STONE > GIANT];[7] that was
a mighty injury. The Víðgymnir <giant> of the ford of Vimur
<river> [= Þórr] struck the ground of the ears [HEAD] off the
gleaming serpent near the waves. Thus [the hall] received
[decoration] inside with memorable pictures. [Marold et al.
2017: 411–17]

Bearing in mind that three half-stanzas and one full stanza
cannot reflect all that was in the poem about this myth, we can recall that we have seen the serpent's baleful gaze in Bragi's poem (st.
4). Here, however, the poet adds Þórr's awful gaze as well (indeed,
perhaps these two half-stanzas were originally the two parts of a
full stanza, artificially broken apart by Snorri to provide examples
of different locutions). Where the poet devotes himself exclusively
to þórr's gaze, to the serpent's gaze, however fearful it is, the poet
adds that the serpent blew poison. From this we might conclude that
Þórr's gaze alone is the equivalent of the serpent's gaze together with
its poison. Here it is worth noting that in Old Norse, one sees out-
ward from one's eyes, as opposed to our notion of the physics, in
which light waves are received by the eyes. Thus the serpent needs
output from eyes and mouth together to match the output of Þórr's
eyes alone.

The next half-stanza has Þórr apparently mocking the terror of
a "heavy-set fat one," clearly the equivalent of the giant in Bragi's
poem, st. 6, and, like that giant, usually identified as Hymir. "Heavy-
set fat one" could be insulting—that is how Edith Marold et al. take
it—but it could probably also refer to the size of the figure in the
carving that the poet is describing. The noun phrase "weighty powerful pull" indicates that þórr has hooked and is pulling up the serpent (the serpent is weighty and Þórr's pull is powerful), and there is

[7] "Reed" here stands either for water or land, and the "bone" of either is a usual kenning
for stone.

no indication of a threat to the fishing line, although we cannot rule out that another now lost stanza presented that motif.

The final stanza is somewhat ambiguous. The blows described in the two half-stanzas could be one and the same ("he struck the serpent's head, and thus he cut it off"), or it could be two blows directed at the serpent ("he struck the serpent's head, and then he cut if off"), or there could be two victims ("he struck the head of the giant in the boat with him, and then he cut off the head of the serpent"). The latter interpretation, which Marold et al. favor, would require two images if the poet limited himself to describing the carvings. "Tester of stone" could be a valid kenning for the serpent if we think of rocks along the coastline, but it might fit better with an ordinary giant, who could be expected to live among stones and rocks (cf. st. 4).

As we have seen, Bragi left the outcome of the duel unresolved (and so do the extant Viking Age images). Úlfr, on the other hand, clearly does resolve the issue, with the death of the serpent; the text is quite clear on this point. What is consistent in the treatment of both Bragi and Úlfr, the one from ninth-century Norway, the other from late tenth-century Iceland, is the persistence of the hook and the terrible gaze of one or both of the opponents. Adding in Qlvir hnúfa's one half-stanza, we see that poets highlighted that betwixt and between moment, when Þórr had the serpent on his hook, and when the two glared balefully at each other.

Úlfr uses kennings for þórr that, for the most part, allude to other victories over giants. Which victory is clear in one of these: in st. 6, Þórr is kenned as "the Víðgymnir <giant> of the ford of Vimur <river>." Vimur was the river Þórr crossed, and perhaps overcame, in the myth of the visit to Geirrøðr and his daughters. The other kennings are unclear but amenable to guesses. "The tester of the peoples of the bone of the earth [ROCK > GIANTS]" may also suggest the Geirrøðr story, since the base word ("tester") might also mean "rowan." Here we perhaps have a pun, insofar as Snorri derives the proverbial expression "the rowan is Thor's rescue" from an incident in that story. "The most powerful killer of the mountain-Gautr <man of the Gautar [GIANT]" could refer to any giant-slaying, but it is tempting to think of a Gautr (that is, an Óðinn; Gautr is a well-known name for Óðinn) of the mountain as some kind of leading figure, perhaps Hrungnir. And "friend of the gods" might just re-call Þjóðólfr's account of Þórr's victory over Hrungnir, for he uses the word for gods found here, *bǫnd*, when he states that the gods willed it that Hrungnir stood on his shield. If I have unpacked these allusions correctly (and I am by no means certain that I have, so al-lusive is this poetry), then Úlfr cleverly put the killing of the World Serpent alongside the killings of Hrungnir, Geirrøðr, and his daugh-ters. Thus he emphasized not the family relationship of Þórr, as Bragi did with his kennings when telling of the hook and gaze, but rather the aftermath, the killing of the monster.

Eysteinn Valdason

Skáldskaparmál records three half-stanzas attributed to one Eysteinn Valdason, who is otherwise completely unknown, which appear to be a fragment of a longer poem about Þórr's encounter with the World Serpent. Although these three stanzas follow one another directly in *Skáldskaparmál*, which is not Snorri's usual practice, it nevertheless makes senses to arrange them in the following order (the second, first, and third in *Skáldskaparmál*), as does Margaret Clunies Ross, the most recent editor of the fragment.

1   The confidant of Sif <goddess> [= Þórr] quickly brought out his fishing gear with the old fellow; we [I] can stir the horn-stream of Hrímnir <giant> [POETRY].

2   The father of Þrúðr <goddess> [= Þórr] stared with piercing eyes at the ring of the steep road [= Miðgarðsormr]; previ-ously the dwelling of the redfish [SEA] surged against the boat.

3   So it came about, that the saithe of the earth [=Miðgarðsormr] made the broad riveted planks slide forward; the fists of the kinsman of Ullr <god> [= Þórr] banged out on the gunwale. [Clunies Ross 2017b: 185–88]

In this arrangement, the first stanza ends with a refrain, the self-referential statement "I can create verse," so we are presumably justified in assuming that the poem had stanzas before here giving the background of the story, perhaps telling us why, as Bragi put it, Þórr wished to test his strength against the serpent. The "old fellow" of this stanza is likely to be the giant who accompanied Þórr on the expedition, Hymir according to the sources that name him. The other stanzas too contain analogues to other versions of the myth, of which the most common, as we have just seen, is Þórr's terrible gaze ("stared with piercing eyes"); here there is no corresponding gaze from the serpent, as elsewhere. Nor is there poison in the air, as in Úlfr's *Húsdrápa*. Instead, it seems, we are closer to the storm implied by Bragi, as the sea rages around the boat. The third half-stanza may imply that the serpent tows the boat, rather as a whale might have done when harpooned from a small boat. We are therefore probably again right in the middle of the scene, with Þórr gazing, the sea crashing, the serpent thrashing, the boat moving. What is new here is the motif of Þórr's fists resounding on the ship or some part of it ("gunwale" could stand for any part of the hull or metonymically for the entire vessel). If Þórr's fists hit and rang out against the hull, we may be obliged to assume that in this version, unlike Úlfr's, he failed to box the serpent's ear. In any case, the poet (or whoever collected his stanzas) leaves us in mid-battle, which is very much within the tradition of the poetics of this myth.

Again, then, we have no outcome, and again we have Þórr kenned with his family relationships: the nuclear family of his wife Sif and daughter Þrúðr, and the affinal relationship with his step-brother Ullr.

Gamli gnævaðarskáld

Skáldskaparmál preserves two half-stanzas from this otherwise unknown poet, one of which appears to be part of a longer poem about
Þórr and the World Serpent, as the first word, "while ("when" in one
manuscript), indicates:

> While the ruler of Bilskirnir <mythical hall> [= Þórr], the one who
> did not plan treachery in his heart, quickly smashed the fish of the
> sea-bed [Miðgarðsormr] with the destruction of the gully-whale
> [GIANT > = Mjǫllnir]. [Clunies Ross 2017c: 189]

The negative suffix translated "not" is found in only one manuscript.
If it is omitted, one infers that some treachery was involved in this version of the encounter, thus perhaps suggesting an intertextual relationship with Hrungnir on his shield, or perhaps Þórr himself in a bridal
gown and veil at the home of the giant Þrymr. Otherwise this version
departs from the majority first in lacking the malevolent gaze of one
or both of the participants, although I am fairly confident that it was
mentioned in one of the stanzas that has not been preserved. But what
is a presence here, and not an absence, is presentation of an outcome.
Gamli agrees with Úlfr in that Þórr killed the beast: he "smashed" the
serpent, or perhaps more literally "tore apart" the beast, here again
kenned as a fish, with Mjǫllnir kenned equally fishily as the destruction of the gully-whale. "Tear apart" is consistent with "behead."

Þórr is kenned as lord of his hall, Bilskirnir, rather than through
any family relationship as in some of the other verses we have seen.
This kenning puts him in Ásgarðr and associates him with the other
Æsir who have halls there (these are enumerated in *Grímnismál*).
The serpent is again kenned as a fish, and in keeping with this kenning, Þórr's hammer is kenned as the destruction of the whale of
land, thus conjoining the doomed serpent with all the giants Þórr
has killed on land.

As I have mentioned, we have no information about Eysteinn and Gamli. Most scholars have placed them in Iceland toward the end of the pre-Christian period, and that is not an unreasonable surmise, given the prominence of Þórr in opposition to the Christian mission and the fact that we have other Þórr poetry from this period. If it holds, one might posit a move from earlier Viking Age Scandinavia (and beyond) to late Viking Age Iceland, from a version of the myth in which the serpent survives, as in Bragi, to a version in which the serpent dies at Þórr's hands, not least because of Eysteinn's version. Nevertheless, since Bragi's verse had to have been passed down in Icelandic oral tradition, both versions were extant in late pre-Christian Iceland. As we shall see, Snorri Sturluson tried to make sense of this discrepancy centuries later, but in pre-Christian Scandinavia people may simply have been aware of the fact that there were different versions of the story.

Indeed, given the distances in time and space and the fluidity of oral tradition, we should perhaps be more surprised at the consistencies in these accounts than the differences. The skalds, like the Viking Age plastic artists, seem to have been interested in the very fact that the two great adversaries met each other at sea, and except for Gamli, from whom we have only twenty-four syllables, they put the locked gazes of the antagonists at the very center of this encounter. Serpents, too, have sharp eyes.

Bright eyes and a powerful gaze indicate high social status and leadership ability (Marold 1998). King Óláfr Haraldsson (later the saint) had them, and they are indeed a trope for good qualities. The gaze of Þórr comes up in other myths as well. For example, toward the beginning of the long account of the visit to Útgarðaloki in *Gylfaginning*, when Þórr discovered that one of his goats was lame (as was mentioned in the previous chapter, the peasant's son Þjálfi had broken the ham-bone to get at the marrow), he was enraged. Snorri describes the rage thus:

There is no need to make a long tale about it, everyone can imagine how terrified the peasant must have been when he saw how Thor was making his brows sink down over his eyes; as for what could be seen of the eyes themselves, he thought he would collapse at just the very sight. [Faulkes 1987: 38]

Þórr controlled his rage and accepted Þjálfi and Rǫskva as his servants in compensation for the damage to the goats. One can also point to the comic moment in *Þrymskviða* (st. 27) when the giant gets a big surprise:

> He bent under the head-dress, he was keen to kiss her,
> instead he sprang back right along the hall:
> "Why are Freyja's eyes so terrifying?
> It seems to me fire is burning from them."

Foolishly, the giant accepts Loki's explanation that "Freyja" has not slept for nine nights, so eager was she to come to Giantlands.

In their language, the skalds typically kenned the serpent as some kind of fish, and they liked to ken Þórr with simple kennings expressing his family relationships, as son, father, husband, kinsman. Thus even if the outcome of the encounter was left unclear, the poets stripped the serpent of his family relationships while stressing those of Þórr. Let us remember that Þórr explicitly makes this into a fishing expedition, for he has fishing gear and bait; fishing is typically undertaken on behalf of a family or community. The solitary serpent meets the representative of the community on a stormy, windswept sea. We should also recall that fishing could be a dangerous business, simply because of the wind and waves.

In two cases Þórr does kill the serpent, and both poets who give us this outcome pass over kennings of family relationship for Þórr and instead ken him as the killer of other giants (Úlfr) or as lord of the glorious estate, Bilskirnir (Gamli). This way of kenning the god is certainly consistent with an outcome of the encounter that is more consistent with the generally agonistic structures of the mythology taken as a whole. As I mentioned in chapter 1, every giant-slaying recapitulates the creation of the cosmos and is therefore a creative act. What I will only add here is that when the encounter is put into the form of a fishing trip, killing (that is, in everyday terms, catching) the fish means that the community eats.

Images

All together, seven images have been put forward as possible illustrations of this myth. Since such identification can only be done on the basis of the extant texts, there is room for doubt, and three of these images are ordinarily left out of the discussion. Of the remaining four, two seem certain, a decorated stone from the churchyard at Hørdum in Thy, Jylland, Denmark, and the decorated rune stone from Altuna, Uppland, Sweden. Nearly as certain, although not unanimously accepted, are a decorated stone from Gosforth, Cumberland, England,[8] and the picture stone from Ardre, Gotland, usually known as Ardre VIII.[9] In considering these images, it should be noted that in some cases archaeologists or state antiquarians have painted in their notions of what the weathered and often quite faint incisions on the stone stand for.

The Hørdum stone is a slab containing an incised image of two human figures facing each other in a boat (figure 2.3).

One holds a fishing line with both hands, taut (as in Bragi, st. 2), and the other holds up something above the fishing line, perhaps an

---

[8] Abram (2011: 36–37), on the other hand, thinks that scholars have been too quick to read this image as Þórr's fishing expedition.

[9] For discussion, see Meulengracht Sørensen (1986); cf. also Kopár (2016). Three other possible images have been suggested, but they are unlikely. They include: "a bronze mount from Solberga, Sweden; the Överjärna runestone (Sö 352), Sweden; and a D-bracteate of uncertain provenance. These associations are, however, highly uncertain (cf. Oehrl 2006: 130–131)" (Kopár 2016: 141, fn. 3).

FIGURE 2.3 Picture stone from Hørdum in Thy, northern Jylland, Denmark. Photo: Lennart Larsen, Nationalmuseet, København.

ax about to cut it (Bragi, st. 6). The foot of the one with the fishing line extends down through the bottom of the boat into the sea. No poet has this motif, but Snorri does; see below. The bait and the shape of the serpent below are no longer clearly visible.

The inscription on the Altuna rune stone is dated to the mid or later eleventh century, and the images presumably date from this time as well (figure 2.4).

FIGURE 2.4 Image on a rune stone at Altuna in Uppland (U 1161, Samnordisk runtextdatabas). Photo: Bengt A. Lundberg, Riksantikvarieämbetet, Stockholm.

The stone stands nearly two meters in height, with incised images as well as the runic inscription. The fishing expedition, located on a narrow side of the stone, depicts a single human figure (not two) in a boat holding an ax or hammer in one hand and a fishing line in the other, with one foot sticking down below the bottom of the boat. The line runs down to what may an ox-head (the bait according to *Hymiskviða* st. 22; see below), and a creature perhaps with three heads encircles the bait. Two other images are to be found above the fishing expedition on this face of the stone: a man on horseback apparently armed with a sword, and a man standing with what might be a raven on his shoulder (and thus might be Óðinn). The runic inscription states that three men raised the stone in memory of two other men who were burned to death. The relationship between the various images and the text resists clarification (treated most recently by Oehrl 2006: 124–28).

The Gosforth "fishing stone" (figure 2.5) is a stone slab with an image most likely from the tenth century.

Here again there are two human figures in a boat, with the mast between them. One apparently holds a fishing line, while the other holds up one arm, perhaps with an ax in it. The fishing line seems to run down under the boat to where a creature appears to bite it. The

FIGURE 2.5 Detail from the so-called fishing stone (Gosforth 6) from St. Mary's church in Gosforth. Photo: Erik Schjeide.

eyes of the fisherman with the line in his hand feature prominently, and the beast's eye may also be discerned.

The picture stone Ardre VIII (figure 2.6) from Gotland is earlier than the other stones (eighth or ninth century).

It is one of the most elaborately decorated picture stones from Gotland, many of which combine a number of images identified as scenes from myth and legend. On this stone we may see Óðinn on

FIGURE 2.6 The picture stone from Ardre on Gotland (SHM 11118:108199). It stands 2.1 meters tall and is conventionally dated to the eighth century. Photo: Ola Myrin, Statens Historiska Museum, Stockholm.

Sleipnir (identified from its eight legs in the upper right). Just below
the ship is an image of two human figures in a tiny boat. On the right
of the boat is what may be the boat's rudder, and to the left a straight
line running slightly downward (the taut fishing line?) attached to
an object that might be understood as the head of an ox. Although
the line appears to run from the bow of the boat, it is possible that
the man in the bow is holding it in some way. Directly below is an in-
distinct image, possibly the serpent. Sune Lindqvist suggested other
possible scenes connected to the myth (1941–1942, 1: 95–96). The
house in the bottom seems to contain an ox and two men leaving
with what may be an ox's head (*Hymiskviða* st. 19); it looks a lot
like the object on the end of the line in the "fishing scene." To the
left of the house are two anthropomorphic figures in a small boat
over what may be a fish net. One of them is spearing a large fish
(whale? Cf. *Hymiskviða* st. 21, where Hymir hooks two whales).[10]
Above that, a man faces a being with multiple heads (cf. Þrívaldi; see
below). This speculative interpretation would create a chain running
clockwise: obtaining the bait; first part of the fishing trip; "the gaze,"
implied by the two figures facing one another and perhaps the otherwise unknown motivation for the fishing expedition (Bragi st. 1);
the World Serpent hooked.

These images show first that the emphasis of this myth when it
was a sacred narrative, that is, during the pre-Christian period, was
the actual hooking of the World Serpent on Þórr's line, before it was
pulled up and before it was or was not killed. Two of the images suggest that the second figure in the boat is threatening either the fisherman or, as Bragi has it, the line. The eyes of the two antagonists
are sometimes prominent as well, as would be consistent with the
skalds' emphasis on the angry gazes of Þórr and the serpent. Three

[10] Emphasizing the net and interpreting the fish as a salmon, Buisson (1976: 63–65)
understands the image as Þórr's capturing of Loki in the shape of a salmon, prior to his
binding (*Gylfaginning*, Faulkes 1987: 48–49). But Snorri has Þórr grasp the salmon, not
spear it, and there is no boat involved.

of the four images have two figures in the boat; Altuna has only one. Among the skalds, Ǫlvir and Gamli do not mention anyone fishing besides Þórr, but in both cases we have only short fragments of what they must have composed. Nevertheless, it is wholly possible that there were versions of the myth in which Þórr acted alone.

In connection with sacred narratives about Þórr, mention should be made of a fragment attributed to Bragi in manuscripts of Snorri Sturluson's *Skáldskaparmál*, for it extremely unusual:

> You have well driven back your draught animals, cleaver asunder of the nine heads of Þrívaldi <giant> [=Þórr], above the famous drink-provider of the drinking party [=Ægir (*ægir* "ocean")]. [Clunies Ross 2017a: 58]

This is a difficult half-stanza. The first phrase may mean "You have well restrained your draft animals," and translation of the last phrase will always be conjectural, since one of the words in the kenning is known from no other source. The kenning "cleaver of the nine heads of Þrívaldi," however, is clear, even if the nine heads conflict to some degree with the name Þrívaldi, which means something like "thrice powerful." What is unusual here is the direct address to Þórr. We have no other direct address to any other god in the poetic corpus, and only two other examples to Þórr. These are from the end of the pagan period in Iceland and praise Þórr in direct address for his giant-slaying. The first is by Vetrliði Sumarliðason:

> You broke the bones of Leikn; you thrashed Þrívaldi; you overthrew Starkaðr; you stepped over the dead Gjálp. [Fulk 2017: 425]

The second is by Þorbjǫrn dísarskáld:

> There was a clang on Keila's crown, you broke all of Kjallandi, you had already killed Lútr and Leiði, you caused Búseyra to bleed, you bring Hengjankjǫpta to a halt, Hyrrokkin had died previously,

yet the swarthy Svívǫr was [even] earlier deprived of life. [Clunies
Ross 2017e: 471]

We know some of these victims from other sources, but most are now
just names (as is, in fact, Þrívaldi), more of them female than male.

Hymiskviða

The eddic poem known as *Hymiskviða* "Hymir's poem" bears this title
in the manuscript fragment of mythological eddic poetry that has
survived alongside the *Poetic Edda*; there it is found under the rubric
"Þórr dragged up the World Serpent [Miðgarðsormr]." Thus whoever wrote this rubic thought of the poem as primarily about Þórr's
encounter with the serpent. It is also, however, as was mentioned in
the previous chapter, about Þórr's winning of a kettle from the giant
Hymir by passing various tests. The fishing expedition is embedded
within this structure, motivated by Hymir's need to get food (st. 17).
This need presumably came about because of Þórr's enormous appetite (st. 16); alone he ate up two of Hymir's oxen.

Scholarship has reached no consensus whatsoever on how
or even whether the parts of *Hymiskviða* fit together and how we
should judge the age of the poem; some scholars stress the obvious
Indo-European analogues (e.g., Schröder 1955, Oosten 1985: 52–
71), while others think the poem in its current form may have been
composed after Snorri wrote his *Edda* (e.g., Meulengracht Sørensen
1986). Given the evidence that the fishing expedition was widely
known during the Viking Age, it is hardly a daring leap to assume
that there was poetry about it in the eddic style, but we cannot be
certain that any of the verses that now exist are identical with verses
that existed during the Viking Age. The similarity of the versions in
the two manuscripts indicates probable stability of text, but we must
accept that we are dealing here not with a sacral text in and of itself
but with an echo of a sacral text.

The poem has a rather chiastic structure. The outside layer is the frame, which consists of the need to acquire the kettle to brew beer for the Æsir and the fact of its acquisition; this frame occupies the opening and closing stanzas. Inside that is the sequence of the travel of Þórr and Týr to and from Hymir's hall, with reference to Þórr's goats (st. 7, 37–38). Within that is the core of the poem. One way to think of this core, and of the relationship between the fishing expedition and the acquisition of the kettle, is as a series of tests, including the fishing expedition. The rest of the tests (again, mentioned in the previous chapter) include breaking the beaker, lifting the kettle, and dispatching the army of giants. Even if one thinks in this way, however, the encounter with the serpent assumes a central position because of the length of the treatment as compared to the other tests.

In the *Poetic Edda*, *Hymiskviða* follows directly on Óðinn's curse to Þórr at the end of *Hárbarðsljóð*: "Go where the monsters'll get you" (st. 60). In context, then, in *Hymiskviða* Þórr in fact goes to where monsters might get him (the verb Óðinn uses is in the present subjunctive, so what he really says is, "Go where the monsters may get you"; more literally even would be, "Go where the monsters may get you whole").[11]

Hymiskviða opens with an epic statement putting it into the distant past but invoking Óðinn only in the Þórr-kenning "Yggr's [=Óðinn's] son" in st. 2. It is Þórr who orders the giant to brew beer, and it is Þórr whom the giant orders, in st. 3, to obtain a kettle for such brewing.

> In bygone days the slaughter-gods had a good bag from hunting,
> they were keen to drink before they got enough;
> they shook the twigs and looked at the augury,
> they found that at Ægir's was an ample choice of cauldrons. [st. 1]

---

[11] These words from *Hárbarðsljóð* appear in the manuscript on the same line as the opening of *Hymiskviða* and the rubric.

There is a kind of division of labor implicit here: Óðinn gets the mead, which is to some extent abstract and metaphorical, and Þórr is to obtain a cauldron, which is material and tangible. This distinction between Óðinn and Þórr is maintained throughout *Hymiskviða*, since Óðinn plays no role in the poem.

As the gods ponder what to do, it is (apparently—see below) Týr who has a plan, and he tells Þórr that they can obtain the kettle if they use deceit: "If, friend, we use trickery to do it" (st. 6). Scholars have found this line puzzling, for deceit hardly enters into the versions of the myth now left to us. This requires playing a semantic game with st. 21, which states that Þórr baited his hook "cunningly"; although it is possible to locate passages in which the word in question refers not to trickery but to skill, they are rare. I would prefer to refer back to the alternate reading of the line from Gamli gnævaðarskáld mentioned earlier: "The one who did nurse treachery in his heart," and to contemplate versions of the story now lost to us in which treachery or trickery did play a role. Of course, there is the simple possibility that using an ordinary fishing trip for cosmic purposes may constitute deceit or treachery, or, as I shall explore, that Þórr uses his appetite in a tricky way.

Over the years, a few observers have seen the possibility that the word *Týr* in st. 4 and 33 may not in fact be the name of the god but rather an extremely rare noun meaning just "god"; formally, the name *Týr* and this rare noun *týr* are the singular form of the plural noun *tívar*, often used in poetry for the collective "gods," and found in fact earlier in st. 4 (it should be pointed out that ordinary Old Norse manuscript writing did not distinguish upper-case and lower-case letters the way we do in modern European writing systems, so there is no way to be certain what the scribe intended, and listeners to an oral performance would also have to determine what the performer intended). The noun *týr* "god" is found once, in the *Haustlǫng* of Þjóðólfr st. 8, in which Loki, who is stuck to and being dragged by the giant Þjazi in the form of an eagle (see chapter 1), is called "the wise *týr*." If the *Hymiskviða* poet meant to use the rare noun for "god," it may have been Loki, rather than Týr, who advised getting the kettle from Hymir and who accompanied Þórr on the journey (von Sydow 1915: 119–20). The reason to pick Loki rather than any other god is not just that Loki does accompany Þórr on his journeys to both Þrymr and Útgarðaloki, but also that Loki is specifically mentioned in st. 37 as having maimed Þórr's goat. An attractive feature of this reading would be to remove the apparent giant paternity of Týr, which hardly fits with the preference of paternal kinship and the tightly structured and seemingly exclusive rules for being accounted a member of the gods or giants. We already know (or perhaps can infer with reasonable confidence) that Loki's father was a giant, elsewhere called Fárbauti. The corpus of Old Norse mythology is so small that we do not see much variation; if Hymir is indeed Loki's father in this text, we would have such a case. If so, the beautiful woman mentioned in the second half of st. 8 could even be Laufey, Loki's mother: "And another woman, all gold-decked, walked forward/with shining brows, bearing beer to her boy."

Whether Þórr's companion is Loki or Týr, the two are stationed behind a column that bursts when Hymir directs his gaze toward it. Given the importance of gazing when Þórr fishes up the serpent, Hymir's frosty and destructive gaze surely functions in an intertextual alliance with that sequence. It aligns him with the serpent and presages what is to come. The poet probably means the audience to gasp for a moment at the line that follows the shattering of the column: "Asunder the pillar splintered at the giant's gaze, just before the cross-beam broke in two" (st. 12), given the homonymity of *áss* "cross-beam" and *áss* "god." Only the following lines, which tells us that kettles fell when the cross-beam broke, clear up the tense ambiguity.

Hymir's gaze is indeed overdetermined here, since when Þórr and his companion cross the floor, the giant directs that same powerful gaze at Þórr. In the end, however, that gaze becomes nothing more than normal sight, as the verb "saw" indicates.

Forward they went, and the ancient giant
turned his gaze on his enemy.
His mind didn't speak encouragingly to him, when he saw
the one who makes the giantess weep walking across the floor.
   [st. 13–14]

It may be tempting to assign Hymir's doleful mood to the fact that he knows that Þórr is likely to eat him out of house and home, as he did with Þrymr and Útgarðaloki, and as he does here, eating two of the three oxen slaughtered. It is tempting to think that Þórr puts his appetite to a purpose in this case, namely to get out on the water after the World Serpent. Such a reading would accord not only with the notion of intent in Bragi's version of the story (Þórr "soon wanted to try his strength against the twisted thing of the earth") but also, as I hinted earlier, with the notion of a plan put forward by Týr/Loki in this poem. The notion of a deliberate flaunting of the appetite with a goal in mind certainly suggests itself in the speed with which Þórr responds to Hymir's doubtless sullen statement to the effect that they will need to set out for more food.

"Tomorrow evening we three must live on
food that we have hunted ourselves."
Thor said he wanted to row out in the bay,
if the bold giant would give him bait. [st. 16–17]

Somehow the explicit number "three," with its masculine gender obviously adding Týr/Loki to the group, is reduced to the dyad of Þórr and Hymir in the actual fishing expedition. A small literature has treated the ambiguity of the kind of food Hymir had in mind, whether animal protein hunted on land or fished in the sea. The reduction of three to two does seem to suggest that Hymir may have had hunting in mind and that Þórr manipulated the situation so as to be able to confront the World Serpent.

Acquiring the bait can be taken as a test, given Hymir's taunt to Þórr: "Go to the herds, if you've the guts for it/mountain-giant-breaker, to look for bait!" (st. 17). Þórr meets this challenge readily, tearing the head off an ox out in the forest (either a sign of the giant's cluelessness—who would herd oxen in a forest?—or an indication of the otherness of this particular all-black ox).

> The young man hastened smartly to the woods,
> there stood an ox, jet-black before him.
> That ogre-slayer broke off from the bull
> the horns' high meadow, tore off its head. [st. 18–19]

Some commentators have fussed over the use of the word "young man" here, but it seems to me to be within the poet's inclination toward exotic expressions and should just be taken, as it often is in *dróttkvætt* poetry, as "warrior."

The next scene is aboard the fishing boat. For a poet who was aiming for a something like a *dróttkvætt* effect in the more narrative eddic form, as he manifestly does with his kennings, it is hardly troubling that he jumps from one scene to another with no transition. The entire sequence of the fishing proper is as follows:

> 20 The lord of goats told the ape's offspring
> to row the launchway-horse out further;
> but the giant said, for his part,
> he wasn't eager to row further out.
>
> 21 The brave and famous Hymir alone caught
> two whales at once on his hook,
> and back in the stern Odin's kinsman,
> Thor, cunningly laid out his line.
>
> 22 The protector of humans, the serpent's sole slayer,
> baited his hook with the ox's head.
> The one whom the gods hate, the All-Lands-Girdler
> from below gaped wide over the hook.

23 Then very bravely Thor, doer of great deeds,
pulled the poison-gleaming serpent up on board.
With his hammer he violently struck, from above
the hideous one, the wolf's intimate-brother's head.

24 The sea-wolf shrieked and the rock-bottom re-echoed,
all the ancient earth was collapsing
***
then that fish sank itself into the sea.[12]

Unlike the skalds, this poet seems to devote each stanza to a slightly different scene in the narrative. Þórr urges the giant to go further out, and the giant is reluctant. The giant fishes up whales, while Þórr is still baiting his hook. Þórr hooks the serpent. Þórr drags up the serpent and smashes it with his hammer. As the cosmos reels, the serpent vanishes into the sea.

What is perhaps most surprising about this presentation is the absence of the gaze, which was so central for the skalds and which the poet had already used back in Hymir's hall. Thus the *Hymiskviða* poet has not only situated the fishing expedition in the context of the acquisition of the kettle, but he has also fundamentally recast the fishing expedition itself, making of it not an image of the moment when the cosmic opponents glare at one another just as the serpent is hooked, but rather a linear narrative about a fishing trip. The cosmic nature of the entire episode, implicit in the verse of the skalds and perhaps located in the adversaries themselves in Ǫlvir's use of the verb "become violent," is set explicitly in the ancient earth itself.

There is no intervention by the "giant helper" here, and, as in Úlfr's version, Þórr gets in a mighty blow to the head of the serpent. The verb used for that blow, translated as a form of "strike" in st. 23

---

[12] The indication of a lacuna in the manuscript before this line is an editorial assumption, on which see below.

(Old Norse *knýja*), is interesting, in that it is frequently used in the context of the sea: people drive (*knýja*) ships through the waves, and they slam (*knýja*) oars into the sea. One scholar aligned the use of the verb here in *Hymiskviða* with its use for the serpent's bashing of the waves in *Vǫluspá* 50 (Wolf 1977: 18), and we might also think of Ǫlvir's use of the verb "become violent" in the fragment we have from him about the encounter.

In describing the encounter, the poet is fond of linguistic juxtapositions: "brave and famous Hymir" and "Thor, doer of great deeds," "the protector of humans," and "the one whom the gods hate," and the kennings "ape's offspring" and "the hideous one" for Hymir as against "Óðinn's kinsman" for Þórr.[13]

In the end, "that fish sank itself into the sea." The translation captures the mediopassive/reflexive form of the verb, with the inevitable effect that, in English, agency is implied, as though the monster were simply retreating into the sea. Another valid translation would be "sank into the sea." The passage is therefore ambiguous, as is the rest of the record regarding the fate of the World Serpent. If the serpent dies, which I think on balance is the more likely interpretation, we must assume that Þórr simply unhooks the corpse and tosses it without ceremony into the sea, as is consistent with the lack of funeral ritual for giants. However, perhaps we should link the lack of ritual in this particular case with Þórr's subsequent hauling up of the boat, the subject of st. 26 and especially 27. This beaching might well be read as an inversion of the launching of Baldr's funeral ship by the giantess Hyrrokkin. If so, the text would reinforce the mythic notion that giants do not get funerals, another indication of the hierarchical relationship between gods and giants. If one follows this

---

[13] In Larrington's translation, "intimate-brother" renders Old Norse *hnitbróðir*, whose first component (*hnit-*) is otherwise unknown. It might just mean something like "complete," but most observers think it is associated with the verb *hnita* "rivet together" and suggests the metaphorical strength of the joining of Loki's two monstrous sons in this context. What I would emphasize here is that riveting is done with a hammer and that Þórr struck a hammer-blow against the serpent's head just one line earlier.

line of speculation, the specific implication would be that Hymir, the glum passenger (st. 25: "the giant wasn't happy as they rowed back") is doomed and that he too will fall without ceremony. This death indeed occurs in st. 36, and there the marvelous kenning for Hymir and his fellow giants, "lava-field whales," with its link to ships and the sea, could possibly also implicate Baldr's funeral.

If, on the other hand, the serpent lives on, wounded, it will continue to threaten gods and men in the mythic present, and that is certainly also a plausible outcome. Since both Bragi and Snorri have a giant cut the line (explicitly named as Hymir in Snorri), and since the stanza in question is a line short, some observers have imagined there to be a lacuna between the cosmic reaction of the earth and the sinking, as Larrington indicates with the suggestion of one or more missing lines. One's reaction to this editorial intervention will depend on how one reads the ambiguous mediopassive preterite: "sinks" or "sinks itself," but given the variation we would expect in an oral tradition, we should not expend a lot of energy worrying about one word in a thirteenth-century manuscript.

Pulling up the boat functions in the core of the poem as one of the tests, and there are two more: break a cup, and then lift the kettle. The breaking of the cup against the giant's head probably calls up images of the giant whom Þórr defeated in a formal duel, namely Hrungnir, who had a stone heart, and perhaps also to Ymir's skull as the sky, if people took the sky not for airy vapor but for something impenetrable, a counterpart to earth. In any case, the significance is clear. The giant laments in st. 32:

> "Great treasures I know I've lost,
> when I see the goblet leaving my lap,"
> the old man announced: "Never again
> can I say, 'ale, you are brewed!'"

Whether this refers to Þórr's passing this test and thus being able to claim the kettle, or the cup as a metonym for the consumption of beer, the effect is the same. And as Hymir and the giants lose the ability to brew beer, the gods gain it.

Snorri

Although Snorri's version cannot qualify as sacred narrative, written as it was by a Christian presenting the myths as more or less historical (see the next chapter), he does offer a number of details that help clarify the myth as presented by the poets. To begin with, Snorri suggests that Þórr may have invoked the treachery implied by most of the manuscript versions of Gamli's stanza, or at least some kind of trickery. The fishing expedition follows the Útgarðaloki story in *Gylfaginning*, and it is motivated as follows:

> Then spoke Gangleri: "Very powerful is Utgarda-Loki, and he uses a great deal of trickery and magic. It is clear that he is powerful when he had men in his following who have great might. But did Thor never get his own back for this?"
>
> High replied: "It is no secret, even among those who are not scholars, that Thor achieved redress for this expedition that has just been recounted, and did not stay at home long before setting out on his journey so hastily that he had with him no chariot and no goats and no companionship. He went out across Midgard having assumed the appearance of a young boy, and arrived one evening at nightfall at a certain giant's; his name was Hymir." [Faulkes 1987: 46]

This assumption of "the appearance of a young lad" may also explain the *Hymiskviða* poet's use of the noun "young man." And yet, although Snorri embroidered on the theme of Þórr as young lad, having the giant first refuse to take Þórr along fishing because of the disguised god's small stature, apparent youth, and presumed inability to withstand the ocean cold, the motif leads nowhere in the greater logic of the story. It does, however, fit nicely in the context of *Gylfaginning*, since in the Útgarðaloki story, Útgarðaloki used magic to make himself and his followers look much larger than Þórr and his companions.

Snorri also invokes the notion of trickery at the moment when Þórr has hauled up the World Serpent:

> And then it is true to say that Thor fooled the Midgard serpent no less than Utgarda-Loki had made a laughing-stock of Thor when he was lifting the serpent up with this hand. [Faulkes 1987: 47]

The feet sticking out underneath the boat in the images on the Hørdum and Altuna stones find an explanation in *Gylfaginning*:

> The Midgard serpent stretched its mouth round the ox-head and the hook stuck into the roof of the serpent's mouth. And when the serpent felt this, it jerked away so hard that both Thor's fists banged down on the gunwale. Then Thor got angry and summoned up his As-strength, pushed down so hard that he forced both feet through the boat and braced them against the sea-bed, and then hauled the serpent up to the gunwale. [Faulkes 1987: 47]

At this point Snorri acknowledges the gaze that figured so prominently in the verse of the skalds. However, he moves it into the personal experience of his readers and listeners:

> And one can claim that a person does not know what a horrible sight is who did not get to see how Thor fixed his eyes on the serpent, and the serpent stared back up at him spitting poison. [Faulkes 1987: 47]

Snorri was now faced with the issue of the outcome of the struggle. The giant cuts the line, and Þórr hurls his hammer after the sinking monster. Snorri has Hár explain that some people say that the hammer decapitated the serpent, "but I think in fact the contrary is correct to report to you that the Midgard serpent lives still and lies in the encircling sea" (Faulkes 1987: 47).

Within the logic of *Gylfaginning*, Hár's opinion makes perfect sense: the serpent escaped Þórr during the Útgarðaloki episode and again in this episode, and the encounter that will resolve the issue will occur at Ragnarøk. Be that as it may, we should avoid falling into the logical trap here that argues that Þórr could not have killed the serpent when he fished it up because the two will fight and kill each other at Ragnarøk. This is a trap because, first, an oral mythology can be expected to have inconsistencies, and, second, because the dead arise to fight at Ragnarøk, and the dead could easily include the serpent.

Although (unlike *Hymiskviða*) the *dróttkvætt* sources say nothing about the subsequent fate of the "giant helper," Snorri has Þórr deliver a fatal punch to Hymir by the ear so that the giant floats upside down near the boat and only his soles are visible. Perhaps Snorri thought that Hymir's head was so very hard because it was made of stone; thus, like ballast, it would stay low in the water and keeps what is attached to it floating upright.

Contemporary understanding of the myth generally follows the interpretation put forward in 1986 by Preben Meulengracht Sørensen. Meulengracht Sørensen thought, first, that the giant was a necessary part of the myth:

> The giant functions in the myth as an, albeit involuntary, helper, i.e. as a mediator between the world of Thór and the world of the monster. The distance between the two poles is made plain by his presence. Through several stages Thór moves away from the cosmos, of which he is the master and to which he belongs, finally to fight the monster in its own element, the ocean depth, which is the opposite of the heavens of the god. [Meulengracht Sørensen 1986: 268]

This opposition informs Meulengracht Sørensen's reading of the development of the myth. Originally, he thought, it indicated cosmic balance, thus explaining why the outcome of the battle was undecided, as in Bragi. Over time, he continued, the narrative came to be influenced by eschatological themes, and thus the serpent could be killed, as in Úlfr. If this is so, then *Hymiskviða* would represent an older stage of the myth, despite presumably acquiring its present form well after the conversion to Christianity.

While there is no way to prove or disprove such a development, the *dróttkvætt* verse, and the images, do not seem to show as much interest in the outcome of the battle as in the fact that Þórr once had the World Serpent on the end of his fishing line and that the two locked gazes. Whether we understand the World Serpent as a force of nature or as a giant made more powerful because of his realm in the sea, the myth of the fishing expedition shows how tenuous the hold is that the gods have over the giants. When he cuts the line, the "giant helper" is in a way like Loki: together with the gods but against them in the end.

Chapter 3

Old Norse Mythology and Learned Medieval Speculation

How could myths about the pre-Christian gods have survived into Christian times and been recorded in manuscripts written by scribes in monasteries, cathedral scriptoria, and the like? They were no longer sacred narratives, so what were they? The short answer for much of Europe is that they were regarded as belonging to national or local history. This view was possible because of at least two theories that flourished in learned and churchly circles, namely demonization and euhemerism.

Demonization simply transformed the pre-Christian gods into Satan or his minions. Óðinn and Þórr were the gods who figured most often in such contexts, and a devil appeared in the form of each to Óláfr Haraldsson the saint to tempt him—to no avail, of course. How deeply established this trope could be is shown by the fact that the Icelandic translator of the life of Saint Martin of Tours by Sulpicius Severis (fifth century) reported that the devil came to Saint Martin in many forms, but most frequently those of Óðinn and Þórr—who can of course hardly have been known to Saint Martin.

An example tied explicitly to the conversion occurs early in *Flóamanna saga* "Saga of the men of Flói" (c. 1290–1350?). The protagonist, Þorgils Örrabeinsfóstri, is one of the very earliest converts to Christianity. Shortly after his conversion, Þórr begins to plague his dreams, upbraiding Þorgils for abandoning him. When Þorgils plans a journey from Iceland out to Greenland, Þórr comes to him in a dream (ch. 26):

> He dreamt that a man came to him, large and red-bearded, and said: "You have decided on a journey, and it will be difficult."
>
> The dream-man looked huge to him.
>
> "It will go ill for you," he said, "unless you believe in me again; then I will watch over you."
>
> Thorgils said he would never want his help again and told him to go away as fast as his legs would take him: "But my journey will go as almighty God wills it."
>
> Then he thought that Thor led him to a certain crag where ocean waves were dashing against the rocks.
>
> "You will find yourself in such waves and never get out, unless you return to me."
>
> "No," said Thorgils, "get away from me, you loathsome fiend. He will help me who redeemed us all with his blood." [Acker 1997: 289]

Even though this saga was written down relatively late, we know that Þórr had a special connection with the deep ocean waters, given the location of his fishing expedition against the World Serpent. The word "fiend" in the last sentence of the text means "demon" or "devil," and it is explicitly juxtaposed to the protection that the new Christian god can offer. But there are more important resonances. In Matthew 4:8–10, Satan takes Christ up on a high mountain and tempts him, but Christ responds: "Begone, Satan! For it is written, 'You shall worship the Lord your God and him only shall you serve'" [RSV translation].

Euhemerism is the theory that the gods had once been humans, or to put it another way, never had been anything other than humans, even if people had worshipped them. The theory takes its name from the Greek writer Euhemerus (Euhemeros) of Messene, who wrote in a now lost work that Zeus was no more than a human king who had declared himself to be a god. Later the theory was expanded to include the possibility that humans were regarded as gods after their deaths and without their own intention. This theory was popular with the Church fathers and was widely known in the Middle Ages from the influence of the writing of Isidore of Seville. We meet it in Scandinavia in some of the earliest historical writings. For example, Ari Þorgilsson inn fróði (the learned) has a kind of appendix to his *Íslendingabók* "Book of Icelanders," c. 1120, deriving kings and also some of his own family from Yngvi (usually a name for Freyr), king of the Turks, and Njǫrðr, king of the *Svíar* "Swedes," with no comment on their divine status. Writing later in the century, the anonymous author of *Historia Norwegie* "History of Norway" has the same information, with a euhemeristic comment:

> King Yngve, who according to a great many was the first ruler of the Swedish realm, became the father of Njord, whose son was Frøy [=Freyr]. For centuries on end all their descendants worshipped these last two as gods. [Ekrem, Mortensen, and Fisher 2003: 75]

In his *Gesta Danorum* (c. 1200), Saxo Grammaticus explained how this happened; it was rather like what Euhemerus reported about Zeus but added the dimension of magic. Three passages present Saxo's view of this process. In the first, early in Book I, Saxo essentially sums up the basic premise of the mythology, the agonism between "giants" and "gods," in the light of euhemerism. He explains that in ancient time there were "three amazing species of wizard, each practising their own miraculous illusions" (Friis-Jensen ed. and Fisher transl. 2015: 41). "The first of these were fellows of monstrous size, whom the ancients called giants" (Friis-Jensen and Fisher 2015: 41). The second were masters of divination and prophecy:

Although they yielded precedence to the former in their frame, they nevertheless excelled them just as much in their brisk acuteness of intellect. Between these and the giants there were interminable battles for supremacy, until the soothsayers won an armed victory over the monster race and appropriated not only the right to rule but even the reputation of being gods. [Friis-Jensen and Fisher 2015: 41]

The third category were the offspring of the first two, and "minds deluded by their legerdemain believed in their deity" (Friis-Jensen and Fisher 2015: 41). At first glance, this category is difficult to explain, but if we consider the euhemerism that he claims for them, they may well be the prehistoric Danish kings and other prominent people referred to as gods ("gods"?) in the first nine of the sixteen books of *Gesta Danorum*.

Indeed, Saxo often refers to the gods simply as gods, sometimes ironically, as in this myth that follows the introduction of Othinus (=Óðinn) later in Book I:

At that time there was a man called Odin who was believed throughout Europe, though falsely, to be a god. . . . The kings of the North, eager to honour his divinity with more enthusiastic worship, executed a representation of him in gold. . . . His wife, Frigg, desiring to walk abroad more bedizened, brought in smiths to strip the statue of its gold. Odin had them hanged and then, setting the image on a plinth, by a marvelous feat of workmanship even made it respond with a voice to human touch. Nevertheless, subordinating her husband's divine honours to the splendour of her own apparel, Frigg submitted herself to the lust of one of her servants; by his cunning she had the effigy demolished and the gold which had been devoted to public idolatry she switched to her personal extravagance. This woman, unworthy of a deified consort, felt no scruples about pursuing unchastity, provided she could more speedily enjoy what she coveted! Need I add anything but to say that such a god deserved such a wife? [Friis-Jensen and Fisher 2015: 53]

Here we see Othinus/Óðinn actually creating a form of idolatry, which is undone by his profoundly misbehaving wife. Today Saxo might put quotation marks around the word *god* in the final sentence, as I did above.

While we do not know this myth from other sources, what follows—his shame drives Othinus into temporary exile—has echoes in ch. 3 of Snorri's *Ynglinga saga*: once when Óðinn stayed away for such a long time that people doubted he would return, his brothers Vé and Vílir divided his property and jointly married Frigg, a motif that is also mentioned in *Lokasenna* st. 26; Óðinn returns shortly thereafter and resumes his authority, property, and marriage to Frigg.

Sometimes Saxo seems to mention the gods outside of the euhemeristic frame, as when, in his version of the myth of Baldr's death, he has Nanna explain why she cannot marry Balderus:

She answered that a god could not possibility wed a mortal, as the huge discrepancy in their natures would preclude any congruous union between them. Sometimes, too, deities were in the habit of revoking their contracts and suddenly fracturing the ties which they had made with inferiors. [Friis-Jensen and Fisher 2015: 151]

However, the euhemeristic explanation is seldom far away. Consider this passage, which follows the conclusion of the Baldr myth, after Othinus has raped a Ruthenian (Russian) princess in order to sire an avenger:

Now the gods, whose principle residence was held at Byzantium, perceived that Odin had tarnished the honour of his divinity by these various lapses from dignity and reckoned he should quit their fraternity. They ensured that he was ousted from his pre-eminence, stripped of his personal titles and worship, and outlawed, believing it better for a scandalous president to be thrown from power than desecrate the character of public religion; nor did they wish to become involved in another's wickedness and suffer innocently for his guilt. Now that the ludicrous behaviour of a high deity had become common knowledge, they were aware that those who had been seduced into paying them holy adoration were exchanging reverence for contempt and growing ashamed of their piety. [Friis-Jensen and Fisher 2015: 169]

Although they live in Byzantium—which agrees with the euhemeristic idea that the Æsir originally lived in the ancient Middle East—there is nothing in this passage until the end that would suggest that the gods are false gods and only really humans.

Finally, in an aside in Book VI, Saxo initiates a discussion of Danish paganism, beginning with a summary of the euhemeristic argument:

At one time certain individuals, initiated into the arts of sorcery, namely Thor, Odin, and a number of others who were skilled at conjuring up marvelous illusions, clouded the minds of simple men and began to appropriate the exalted rank of godhead. Norway, Sweden, and Denmark were ensnared in a groundless conviction, urged to a devoted worship of these frauds, and infected by the smirch of their gross imposture. [Friis-Jensen and Fisher 2015: 379–81]

Saxo goes on to argue that the weekday names prove that the Danish gods cannot be identical with the Roman gods, since Mercury, who should be equated with Óðinn, was the son of Jupiter, who was to be equated with Þórr, whereas Þórr, according to Danish popular belief, was not the father but the son of Óðinn.

Saxo was the first Scandinavian mythographer. Snorri Sturluson was the second. In the opening chapters of his *Ynglinga saga*, the first of the sagas in his *Heimskringla*, Snorri writes about the emigration from Troy of a tribe call Æsir, which he connects with the word *Ásía* "Asia," although it is the usual word for pagan gods, as we have seen in previous chapters, and never is connected with Asia except in this euhemeristic context. Their king, Óðinn, leads them. Even back in Asia his followers had begun to call upon him when they were in trouble at sea or on land, and seeing his success in battle, they came to believe that he had a special right to victory (as might a god of war like Óðinn). Foreseeing that his future lies in the North, Óðinn leads his people through Germany and Denmark to Sigtuna in Sweden, where they settle. Óðinn is extremely skilled in all forms of magic:

> Most of these skills he taught the sacrificial priests. They were next to him in all manner of knowledge and sorcery. Yet many others learned a great deal of it; hence sorcery spread far and wide and continued for a long time. People worshipped Óthin and his twelve chieftains, calling them their gods, and believed in them for a long time thereafter. [Hollander 1964: 11]

The twelve chieftains are of course the other Æsir whom we usually know as gods.

What Snorri is attempting here is an explanation for the pre-Christian religion and mythology of Scandinavia. Here it may be worth noting that the "magic and sorcery" of Óðinn, as Snorri describes it in ch. 7 of *Ynglinga saga*, accords with the abilities of the *noaidi*, the shaman-figure of the Sámi, the neighbors of the Scandinavians in Norway and Sweden. This too may have constituted a form of euhemerism: Óðinn had the abilities of a (human) Sámi shaman, and his followers thought this made him god-like and finally a god. It must also be mentioned that there is reason to believe that people really did worship kings and perhaps other ancestors after they had died, and such genuine pagan practice could have strengthened the application of the theory of euhemerism.

Snorri's theory of euhemerism also runs throughout his *Edda*, beginning with the *Prologue*. The opening of Snorri's *Edda*—that is, of the *Prologue*—a book which has gained fame outside of Iceland primarily as a repository of Old Norse mythology, is: "Almighty God created heaven and earth and all things in them" (Faulkes 1987: 1).[1] However, Snorri goes on, ultimately people forgot the name of God. Nevertheless, through observing nature, they groped their way to an uninformed monotheism.

> And so they believed that he ruled all things on earth and in the sky, of heaven and the heavenly bodies, of the sea and the weathers. But so as to be better able to give an account of this and fix it in memory, they then gave a name among themselves to everything, and this religion has changed in many ways as nations became distinct and languages branched. [Faulkes 1987: 2]

With this somewhat obscure passage, Snorri seems to be trying to explain not only the diversity of paganism in his own time (besides Old Norse mythology, he probably knew the paganism described in early Christian writings, as well as something of Sámi religion), but also how the unenlightened monotheism he imagined after people forgot the name of god could have grown into polytheistic systems, such as Old Norse mythology. In what follows in the *Prologue*, Snorri relies on the idea of differing names for the same individual to link Scandinavia with Troy and world history. In order to make this work, he upends some of the system of Old Norse mythology and makes Þórr the father of Óðinn.

> The name of one king there [Troy] was Munon or Mennon. He was married to the daughter of the high king Priam; she was called

---

[1] Actually, one manuscript has a header above this text, explaining that Snorri is the author and describing the contents.

Troan. They had a son, he was called Tror; we call him Thor. [Faulkes 1987: 3]

This Tror was raised in and ultimately ruled over Thrace, of which Snorri says, "We call this Thrudheim" (Faulkes 1987: 3)—Þórr's residence in the mythology.

> Then he travelled through many countries and explored all quarters of the world and defeated unaided all berserks and giants and one of the greatest dragons and many wild animals. In the northern part of the world he came across a prophetess called Sibyl, whom we call Sif, and married her. [Faulkes 1987: 3]

Here is much of the mythology of Þórr recast into Snorri's version of Trojan history: the historical Þórr, called Tror by the Trojans, traveled frequently, killed monsters, including a great dragon (doubtless the World Serpent) and married Sif.

Tror and Sibyl—that is, Þórr and Sif—beget a genealogical line of sons that includes many names "whom we call" by some Nordic name form, and it ends after sixteen generations with Woden—"it is him that we call Odin" (Faulkes 1987: 3); the name form Woden makes it clear that Snorri's model for this kind of thinking was originally Anglo-Saxon genealogical material.

Now the euhemerism we have already seen in *Ynglinga saga* comes into play. With the gift of prophecy, which he shares with his wife Frigida "whom we call Frigg," Óðinn discovers that his future lies to the north, and he sets off with a great following. "And whatever countries they passed through, great glory was spoken of them, so that they seemed more like gods than men" (Faulkes 1987: 4). Similarly:

> And such was the success that attended their travels that in whatever country they stopped, there was then prosperity and good peace there, and everyone believed that they were responsible for it

because the people who had power saw that they were unlike other people they had seen in beauty and wisdom. [Faulkes 1987: 4]

"Prosperity and good peace" was a ritual formula for one of the most important things people sought when they sacrificed to the gods, according to our sources, so in these lines Snorri implies that Óðinn and the other Æsir were the recipients of sacrifice. But here, too, he stops short of saying outright that they were taken to be gods. Nor does he invoke the magic of *Ynglinga saga*, and of Saxo, that deceived people into taking Óðinn and the Æsir for gods. In this version of the euhemerism, it is rather "because the people who had power saw that they were unlike other people in beauty and wisdom" (Faulkes 1987: 5).

As they travel, Óðinn appoints kings over lands through which they pass: East Saxony, Westphalia, France, Jylland and Denmark, and finally Sweden, where Óðinn settles in Sigtúnir (a few kilometers from today's Sigtuna). He establishes Sæmingr as the head of the dynasty in Norway and Yngvi in Sweden.

It is against this euhemeristic background that the first section of Snorri's Edda, *Gylfaginning*, should be understood. The title means "Deluding of Gylfi," and Gylfi was introduced in the *Prologue* as a Swedish king who, "when he learned of the arrival of the men of Asia (who were called Æsir), he went to meet them and offered Odin as much power in his realm as he wished himself" (Faulkes 1987: 4). Clearly Gylfi was one of those "people of power" who were impressed by the beauty and power of the Æsir. Gylfi's deluding occurred when he met with the Æsir and had a conversation with three of them. Here is how it is put early in *Gylfaginning*:

> King Gylfi was clever and skilled in magic. He was quite amazed that the Æsir-people had the ability to make everything go in accordance with their will. He wondered whether this could be as a result of their own nature, or whether the divine powers they worshipped could be responsible. [Faulkes 1987: 7]

Gylfi assumes a disguise and, calling himself Gangleri (perhaps "Tired from walking"), he pays them a visit, but the Æsir "were the wiser in that they had the gift of prophecy ... and prepared deceptive appearances for him" (Faulkes 1987: 7). He sees an impressively large hall, with many rooms and many people, "some engaged in games, some were drinking, some were armed and fighting" (Faulkes 1987: 8).[2] Then he saw three thrones, one above the other. In the lowest sits the king, whose name is Hár "High"; above him sits Jafnhár "Just as High," and above him in turn is Þriði "Third." This image is charmingly captured in an image in the Uppsala manuscript of Snorri's Edda from c. 1300 (figure 3.1).

These are all names of Óðinn, and the hall of Hár is Óðinn's hall in the mythology.

What follows is a dialogue in which Gylfi/Gangleri puts questions and one of the throne-sitters, most often Hár, gives an answer, usually a narrative, that is, a myth. Such dialogues were common in didactic texts in the Middle Ages, and because usually it is a disciple or young man who puts questions to a master, here a prehistoric Swedish king is presented as a puerile pupil before the Trojans and their trickery and magic. The questions Gylfi/Gangleri poses essentially invoke the mythology from the creation of the cosmos to its destruction and rebirth—the subject of chapter 1— but it begins with a question about the "highest and most ancient of all gods" (Faulkes 1987: 8). Thus Gylfi appears to be one of those people Snorri mentioned in the *Prologue* who grasped the essence of monotheism even though they could not articulate it. Certainly there is much in what Gylfi/Gangleri hears in response to this question that any Christian would recognize. This highest and most ancient god, who bears a number of Óðinn names, the first of which is Alfǫðr "All-father," has existed for all times, created heaven and

---

[2] Drinking and fighting characterize the life of the *einherjar*, Óðinn's warriors in Valhǫll, about which Gylfi will hear.

FIGURE 3.1 Illustration of the dialogue between Gylfi/Gangleri and the Æsir Hár, Jafnhár, and Þriði, in *Gylfaginning*, in Codex Upsaliensis of *Snorra Edda* (vellum leaf 50, DG 11, Uppsala Universitetsbibliotek). The words just above Gylfi's mouth read: "Gangleri asks." Photo: Uppsala Universitetsbibliotek, Uppsala.

earth, and created human beings and endowed them with souls. The righteous dwell with him, but the wicked go to Hel and then to Niflhel "Fog-hell,"[3] which is down in the ninth world. As Snorri

---

[3] As we saw in chapter 1, according to Snorri, Hel ruled over the underworld; however, there was also a noun, *hel*, referring to a world of the dead, and this term was even sometimes used for the Christian hell; and thus Snorri is probably engaging in some word play here. In

wrote in the *Prologue*, people came up with many names when they forgot the name of god.

Immediately thereafter, we are plunged into the mythology. Gylfi/Gangleri's questions, and the Æsir's answers, take us from the cosmogony and anthropogony through cosmology to a survey of the important gods and (at far shorter length) goddesses; through Freyr's marriage to Gerðr and life in Valhǫll; to the building of the fortification around Ásgarðr and the siring of Sleipnir; to Þórr's visit to Útgarðaloki—the longest narrative in *Gylfaginning*—and to Hymir, where he fished up the World Serpent; to the death of Baldr and vengeance taken upon Loki; and finally to Ragnarøk and its aftermath. Thereafter, Gylfi/Gangleri hears loud noises and finds himself standing in a forest, the hall having vanished.

Gylfi's delusion certainly consisted of the vision of the nonexistent hall, but it also probably consisted of the information he learned in it, or rather how that information was manipulated. For the last paragraph of *Gylfaginning* reports that the Æsir decided to assign the names in the stories they had just told (myths they had just recounted) to the people and places that were there in Sweden, "so that when long periods of time had passed men should not doubt that they were all the same, those Æsir about whom stories were told above and those who were now given the same names" (Faulkes 1987: 57). In other words, they consciously performed a kind of euhemerism by taking on the names of ancient gods. It seems likely that here Snorri is putting forth a theory for the origin of Nordic pre-Christian religion: it was imported from Asia and taken up by Swedes who had been tricked. In this context we should recall the statement in the *Prologue* about Gylfi ceding land and power within his realm to Óðinn. He had clearly been deeply deceived.

The structure of the exposition of the mythology in *Gylfaginning* follows to some degree that of *Vǫluspá*, mentioned in the

---

most contexts, *niflhel* seems to be no more than a poetic variation for the realm *hel*. Its force here is to reduce somewhat the analogy with Christian cosmology.

Introduction and chapter 1. Snorri clearly knew some version of that poem, for he has the Æsir cite quotations from it, along with extensive quotations from two other eddic poems, *Vafþrúðnismál* and *Grímnismál*, and one stanza of *Skírnismál*,[4] as well as verses from what we assume are now lost eddic poems. The stanzas they cite sometimes do not accord with the versions known from other manuscripts. At a bare minimum, these alternative readings, along with the others within specific eddic poems, show that variation was part of the tradition. As has been mentioned, many scholars now also accept that we are seeing variation that is consistent with oral transmission and performance.

The mythological narratives in *Gylfaginning*, and those of *Skáldskaparmál*, of which more in a moment, are the clearest presentation of Old Norse mythology this side of modern handbooks; indeed, what Snorri was attempting was quite similar to what the author of a modern handbook must do: he was balancing his sources, clarifying in places, systematizing, and sometimes admitting the existence of irreconcilable variation in his sources, as with the issue of the outcome of Þórr's fishing expedition, discussed in the previous chapter. Of course, a modern author would not set such an account in the form of a dialogue between a prehistoric Swedish king and a group of immigrant wizards, but a modern author would not be compelled to confront the fact that the ancient myths were sacred texts within an abandoned and forbidden religious system practiced by his or her recent ancestors. Snorri (not the Æsir) faced this issue openly in an early part of Skáldskaparmál:

> But these things have now to be told to young poets who desire
> to learn the language of poetry and to furnish themselves with a
> wide vocabulary using traditional terms; or else they desire to be
> able to understand what is expressed obscurely. Then let such a one

---

[4] This poem recounts the wooing of Gerðr on Freyr's behalf by his servant, Skírnir. Snorri summarizes the plot rather briefly and then quotes the final stanza from the poem.

take this book as scholarly inquiry and entertainment. But these stories are not to be consigned to oblivion or demonstrated to be false, so as to deprive poetry of ancient kennings which major poets have been happy to use. Yet Christian people must not believe in heathen gods, nor in the truth of this account in any other way than that in which it is presented at the beginning of this book, where it is told what happened when mankind went astray from the true faith, and after that about the Turks, how the people of Asia, known as Æsir, distorted the accounts of the events that took place in Troy so that the people of the country would believe that they were gods. [Faulkes 1987: 64–65]

Here we have the motivation for Snorri's euhemerism: to enable people to understand and compose poetry. The kind of poetry he has in mind here is *dróttkvætt* poetry. Indeed, the Æsir in *Gylfaginning* quote only eddic poetry, whereas *Skáldskaparmál* is only about *dróttkvætt* poetry. Part of the distinction in the minds of Snorri and his readers was that eddic poems supposedly took place in prehistory in mythical space or the semi-mythical locations of heroic poetry, whereas the skalds whom Snorri knew were historical figures who very often composed about historical events and historical kings in Scandinavia and Scandinavian England. Despite this distinction, however, there are several *dróttkvætt* poems that recount myths, as we have seen in the previous chapter, and these verses are to be found in *Skáldskaparmál*.

Like *Gylfaginning*, *Skáldskaparmál* begins with a euhemeristic premise, namely that a person called Ægir or Hlér, from the Danish island of Læssø ("Hlér's island"), who was very skilled in magic, set out to visit Ásgarðr, "and when the Æsir became aware of his movements, he was given a great welcome, though many things had deceptive appearances" (Faulkes 1987: 59); the only such thing Snorri mentions is swords that shine like lights. Ægir is seated next to Bragi, and their conversation constitutes the didactic dialogue.

We must take these Æsir as the historical immigrants. Ægir would be the first settler on Læssø, and the Bragi with whom he drinks and converses would be the historical poet Bragi. But Snorri has his own deceptive appearances at work here, since in the mythology Ægir is a giant probably associated with the ocean (the meaning of the noun *ægir*), and according to Snorri there was, alongside the historical Bragi, a god of poetry with the same name; as we have seen in the Introduction, they must be the same individual.

Bragi begins by telling Ægir a myth, namely that of the alienation and recovery of Iðunn, including the death of the giant Þjazi and compensation awarded to his daughter Skaði. After an aside about Þjazi's heritage, Ægir asks Bragi about poetry, and this elicits the narration of the myth of the origin of the mead of poetry, from settlement of the war between the Æsir and Vanir to Óðinn's theft of the mead of poetry. Ægir switches to some technical questions about poetic language, and at that point we find the statement quoted earlier about the purpose of the book. At this point the didactic dialogue frame ceases to be applied consistently, and for that reason this section of *Skáldskaparmál* has been known as *Bragaræður* "Bragi's conversations." In one manuscript it is appended directly to *Gylfaginning* and separated by other material from *Skáldskaparmál* proper; in others a few of the myths are relocated to later in *Skáldskaparmál* and are placed in Bragi's mouth. This difference is inconsequential.

The partial use of the didactic dialogue frame in *Skáldskaparmál*, as opposed to its fluent and motivated use in *Gylfaginning*, has led to the attractive hypothesis that *Skáldskaparmál* was composed first and that Snorri perfected the form in *Gylfaginning*. One implication of this hypothesis is that the entire work was composed in reverse order: first *Háttatal* "Enumeration of Meters," which consists of a praise poem Snorri had composed in honor of the boy king Hákon Hákonarson and his guardian the Jarl Skúli,[5] equipped with

---

[5] The term *jarl* is cognate with English *earl*. Originally it referred to a chieftain, sometimes ruling over a considerable realm, but as the institution of kingship grew, the jarl became officially subservient to the king and finally an officer in the king's court.

a didactic dialogue about the metrics. Snorri visited the Norwegian court in 1218–1220, and it is likely that he composed the poem and the metrical treatise just after that time. *Háttatal* contains 101 stanzas demonstrating one hundred variations of meter or rhetoric, and we still use much of the vocabulary Snorri introduced when we talk about Old Norse poetry. *Skáldskaparmál* complements the highly technical largely metrical presentation of *Háttatal* by focusing on the language of poetry—that is, in the case of this poetry, the kennings and *heiti* (poetic nouns) sometimes referred to as *ókennd heiti* "un-kenned nouns." The embedded narratives help explain kennings by telling some of the stories behind them, but far from all of them. *Gylfaginning* fills this gap, and also provides, along with the *Prologue*, the intellectual frame in which the entire work is to be read; according to this theory of reverse order of composition, the *Bragarœðr* would have to have been composed last, since it refers back to "the beginning of this book" and makes explicit claims about the value of the material and its separation from pre-Christian religion.

The myths told by Bragi, and simply recounted later in *Skáldskaparmál* in what is surely Snorri's voice, are similar in style and tone to those recounted in *Gylfaginning*. But they are rare; most of the text consists of verses, over five hundred of them if one includes the *þulur* (versified lists) that conclude the work in several manuscripts. Most of the other four hundred or so verses are, as it were, excerpted from the poems in which they appear. As an example, here is the first set from the main manuscript of Snorri's *Edda*;[6] it is hardly coincidental that the first topic is Óðinn and the first locution exemplified is "All-father."

---

[6] GkS 2367, 4to, also known as Codex Regius of Snorri's *Edda*. The following discussion primarily follows this manuscript, and the reader should bear in mind that the various manuscripts of *Skáldskaparmál* vary, sometimes significantly. These variations will for the most part remain outside the discussion here.

We shall present further examples of how major poets have found it fitting to compose using these kinds of terms and kennings, as for instance Arnor, the earls' poet, who gives Odin the name All-father:

> Now plan I to tell men—long takes my pain to ease—the virtues of the hostile earl—All-father's malt surf [the mead of poetry] pounds [resounds].

Here he also calls his poetry All-father's malt-surf. Havard the halt said this:

> Now for sea-steeds' [ships'] trunks [warriors] there is eagles' flight over land in store [i.e. the birds of prey are gathering, a battle is taking place]. I guess they are getting Hanged-god's [Odin's] hospitality [in Val-hall] and rings [plunder].

Viga-Glum said this:

> The host with Hanged-Tyr's [Odin's] hoods [helmets] held back—they thought it not pleasant to venture—from going down the slopes.

Ref said this:

> Often the kind man brought me to the raven-god's [Odin's] holy drink [instructed me in poetry]. Baldr [this man] of the prow-land's [seas'] flashes [gold] is departed from the poet [i.e. dead]. [Faulkes 1987: 66]

Another two dozen verses follow these, all giving examples of how Óðinn may be kenned. The kennings in the three verses above would be unintelligible without knowledge of the myths of the acquisition of the mead of poetry and of Óðinn's self-sacrifice, along with the mythological knowledge that Óðinn possesses two ravens, Huginn and Muninn (perhaps "Thought" and "Memory"); they fly about and bring knowledge back to him.

Perhaps more typical is the way Snorri presents Þórr several pages later, namely by beginning with a list of kennings:

> How shall Thor be referred to? By calling him son of Odin and Iord, father of Magni and Modi and Thrud, husband of Sif, stepfather of Ull, ruler and owner of Miollnir and the girdle of might, of Bilskirnir, defender of Asgard, Midgard, enemy and slayer of giants and troll-wives, killer of Hrungnir, Geirrod, Thrivaldi, lord of Thialfi and Roskva, enemy of the Midgard serpent, foster son of Vingnir and Hlora. [Faulkes 1987: 72]

A significant portion of the kennings listed in this format are not to be found in the attested poetry, such as the supposed Þórr-kenning "foster son of Vingnir and[/or] Hlóra," a kenning we no longer understand. This is likely to be just one more piece of evidence indicating that we no longer possess all the myths that were in circulation (let alone all the variations that were in circulation of the myths we do know). In addition, some of the kennings offered for figures who do not (at least in the texts we have) play a large role, such as Sif or Iðunn, are not actually attested. This too could be a result of texts not surviving, but we cannot rule out that Snorri invented these kennings (which are perfectly comprehensible and plausible, such as "mother of Þrúðr" for Sif or "wife of Bragi" for Iðunn). Even if Snorri did invent them, all it shows is that poets, including Snorri himself, knew how to fashion kennings out of mythological material.

As was just mentioned, the first kennings Snorri runs through refer to Óðinn. The second category is poetry, and then follow the rest of the gods, starting with Þórr. In most manuscripts, the next section is a prose recounting of Þórr's duel with Hrungnir, followed by the first of three citations of mythological verses not excerpted but presented in order as part of a poem, namely a passage from Þjóðólfr ór Hvini's *Haustlǫng* "Autumn-long" (tenth century) telling the same myth. The second such passage, from Eilífr Goðrúnarson's *Þórsdrápa* "Þórr's poem,"[7] takes up and follows immediately upon a prose summary of the myth of Þórr's visit to the giant Geirrøðr. Thereafter comes a section on kennings for goddesses, and following discussion of Iðunn, Snorri inserts another passage from *Haustlǫng*, this one about the loss and recovery of that goddess.

The next categories taken up are the sky, the earth, the sea, the sun, wind, fire, winter, and summer. These have mythological importance. The sky, earth, and sea were made from the body of Ymir, and the sun is animate and probably to be regarded as a goddess. Snorri also presents wind, fire, summer, and winter as animate beings; for example, wind is "son of Fornjótr," and fire is "brother of wind and of Ægir."

Next is a discussion, without verse examples, of how to ken human beings, followed by a long section about kennings for gold, including narration of the myth of Sif's golden hair and the other treasures that the dwarfs created along with it. This section of gold kennings contains in some manuscripts several narratives from heroic legend: the so-called "Burgundian cycle," that is, the stories of Sigurðr the dragon slayer and his murder; Guðrún's gruesome murder of her husband Atli as revenge for his killing of her brothers (before killing him and burning down the hall, she kills their sons and feeds Atli their hearts, offering him mead to wash it down in drinking cups made of the boys' skulls); and finally the doomed expedition of Hamðir, Sǫrli, and Erpr against Jǫrmunrekkr. Following this long narration, Snorri quotes a section from Bragi's *Ragnarsdrápa* about the attack on Jǫrmunrekkr. The following account of Fróði's mill, found in two manuscripts, has appended to it the eddic poem *Grottasǫngr*. Another long narrative tells of the hero Hrólfr kraki. The gold kennings morph into kennings for men and women that use the

---

[7] The term *drápa* refers to a *dróttkvætt* poem divided into sections through the use of one or more refrains. It was the most elaborate and high-status kind of poem a skald could compose.

concept of gold, and then come weapons and battle, followed by the story of the eternal battle of Heðin and Hǫgni and the quotation of a chunk of verse telling the same legend from Bragi's *Ragnarsdrápa*. The final category taken up is Christ; *dróttkvætt* poetry survived the conversion to Christianity and was easily and sometimes beautifully put to use for Christian topics.

Thus there is a progression in the categories for which Snorri provides kennings, from the gods, to the humans of heroic legend, and finally to Christ. It is clearly intended as a historical progression, from the prehistory of the gods through the legendary history of the heroes to the contemporary Christianity. Although the gods coexist with heroes insofar as they initiate the "Burgundian cycle," it seems clear that Snorri and presumably his audience regarded them as having lived in the distant past. How far distant? *Skáldskaparmál* tells us explicitly:

> Why is gold called Frodi's meal? The origin of that is this story, that there was a son of Odin called Skiold, from whom the Skioldungs are descended. His residence and the lands he ruled over were in what is now called Denmark, but was then known as Gotland. Skiold had a son called Fridleif who ruled the territory after him. Fridleif's son's name was Frodi. He succeeded to his father's kingdom in the period when the emperor Augustus established peace over all the world. It was then that Christ was born. [Faulkes 1987: 106–7]

Snorri did not invent this information. He was following a now lost saga about the Danish kings, *Skjǫldunga saga*, which we have in a seventeenth-century Latin paraphrase from the Icelandic antiquarian Arngrímur Jónsson.[8] *Skjǫldunga saga* (or rather Arngrímr's

---

[8] The information about Denmark being called Gotland is not in Arngrímur's paraphrase, but it was fairly common in the Icelandic Middle Ages. Scholars assume that the name Gotland does not refer to the Baltic island but perhaps to Jylland.

paraphrase) begins with the so-called learned prehistory, in which Óðinn comes out of Asia to the North and establishes kingdoms there, so we can surmise that Snorri intends his remarks here to be understood in a euhemeristic frame. Be that as it may, if we assign twenty-five years or so to each generation, Snorri, following *Skjǫldunga saga*, puts Óðinn, as the great-grandfather of Fróði, in the middle of the first century BCE.

This euhemeristic theory, which informs all of Snorri's *Edda*, made it possible for learned men like Snorri and Saxo Grammaticus to record the mythology, and there is no reason to believe that they were not recording some form of the pre-Christian belief system. As was mentioned earlier, we encounter the theory as early as the first Icelandic vernacular history, that of Ari Þorgilsson the learned from the early twelfth century, and it is certainly not impossible that it figured in the well-known but lost work about Norwegian kings by his elder predecessor, Sæmundr Sigfússon (to whom the *Poetic Edda* was wrongly attributed in the seventeenth century).

With the theory of euhemerism we have the *how* of the preservation of Old Norse mythology centuries after the conversion, but we do not have the *why*. Although the conversion to Christianity focused on elimination of pre-Christian ritual and its replacement with Christian ritual, perhaps especially baptism and Christian burial,[9] rather than on belief, we may still wonder why stories about the pre-Christian gods would continue to be told.

One explanation might be the simple entertainment value of the myths, which have fascinated and enthralled readers and listeners in many different literary and social environments (a topic to be

---

[9] This statement would find support in the Christian laws section of the main manuscript of *Grágás*, the Christian law code of the Icelandic free state: it begins with a detailed series of provisions regarding baptism—the priest's duties, what to do if the priest is not at hand, and so forth—to the requirement for Christian burial, and how it is to be applied in various circumstances. Thereafter come provisions about churches, priests, bishops, the observation of holy days, and so forth. The only reference to belief is somewhat oblique: a requirement that everyone must know the Lord's Prayer and the Credo.

taken up in the next chapter). Acquisition stories and fights with monsters easily cross social and literary boundaries, and the shape-changing and magic are not unlike the popular genres such as fairy tales and ballads. A medieval example of the entertainment value of the myths, possibly relevant to this explanation for their retention, is provided in connection with a new poetic form that emerged in Iceland in the middle of the thirteenth century: the *rímur*, literally "rhymes," longish narrative poems adapting older meters but regularly making use of end-rhyme. Poets composed *rímur* on many topics, including romances and old heroic tales; among the medieval *rímur* are two recast myths, namely *Lokrur*, on Þórr's visit to Útgarðaloki, and *Þrymlur*, on Þórr's recovery of his hammer from the giant Þrymr. This latter myth also turns up recast as a ballad in Danish, Norwegian, Swedish, and possibly also Faroese tradition. Although there are no medieval recordings of the ballad, it surely attests the entertainment value of the story, probably from during the Middle Ages. Since the myths still fascinate us today, it is tempting to subscribe to this theory, but it hardly seems sufficient to explain the extremely thorough and deep knowledge of the entire mythological system as a functioning whole.

A second answer might be that the myths could have explained physical remains of the old religion that had survived from the Viking Age. These could have included such diverse phenomena as theophoric place names (those containing the names of gods, such as Torsåker "Þórr's field"); images that had survived from the Viking Age, such as those of Þórr's fishing expedition, or the Gotland picture stones, or, presumably, a vast number of wood carvings that are now lost; and other surviving artifacts, such as the so-called Þórr's hammers, or such phallic figurines as those from Södermanland, Sweden (usually taken to be Freyr; see figure 3.2 and figure 3.3).

We tell stories in a physical environment, and that environment contributes significantly to what we tell. Still, this explanation too might not explain how the entire system of the mythology survived, rather than individual myths.

FIGURE 3.2 Bronze statuette from Rällinge in Södermanland (SHM 14232:109037). Photo: Alamy.

A third explanation, and one that would explain the survival of knowledge of the mythological system, could be that the myths were "good to think with," an expression we owe to the eminent myth scholar Claude Lévi-Strauss. Even cross-culturally, one could assume that the models of a scheming amoral magician and sage like Óðinn, a strong and tough protector of society's values like Þórr, or a deeply ambiguous figure like Loki would have resonance, as would narratives about dubious agreements, such as the binding of the wolf,

FIGURE 3.3 Statuette from Lunda in Södermanland, Sweden (SHM 34914:363607). Photo: Gabriel Hildebrand, Statens Historiska Museum, Stockholm.

or about death and grief, as in Baldr's death. However, in the case of Old Norse mythology, it is apparent that the Old Norse myths formed frames of reference for thought and behavior that were still powerful in the late twelfth and early thirteenth century, when they were recorded in literary texts—frames of reference that obviously existed outside of and beyond the religious belief system, since the literature was produced by Christians. To take an obvious example,

FIGURE 3.4 Bronze mounting with a pair of he-goats from Tissø, Jylland, Denmark, dated to the late Iron Age, and perhaps relevant to Þórr's goats. Photo: Pia Brejnholt/Pre-Christian Cultsites, Nationalmuseet, København.

the blood-brother oath was a significant plot element in more than one of the so-called sagas of Icelanders—narratives about the early history of the island up through the conversion period. Blood-brother oaths were meant to bind unrelated men to each other as though they were brothers, but they did not create relationships between families. How strong can such a bond actually be? One way to think about the matter might have been in light of the blood-brother oath between Loki and Óðinn. In the sagas blood-brother oaths generally unravel.

The most obvious intersection between medieval Icelandic life and the mythology would be through the system of dispute resolution, which in real life involved personal strength and the strength of one's supporters. As in the mythology, the stronger and smarter had their way, and the weaker and less strategically adept had to accept their lots. But when two sides were of approximately equal strength, as also in the mythology, conflict was difficult to manage, and attacks on property could escalate to assault and murder. Medieval Iceland had a system of bloodfeud to help manage such violence through rules that everyone knew. When adhered to, these slowed the pace of conflict, thus mitigating it to a degree, and kept open warfare at bay (of course, bloodfeud was impossible when there was a killing within a family). The mythology offered a chilling warning about what could happen when individual killings escalated into all-out war: nothing less than the destruction of the world. Echoes of the mythology were surely audible in medieval Iceland when the struggles between powerful chieftains and their followers escalated into what amounted to a civil war that raged from c. 1220 until 1262–1264, when Iceland fell into the realm of the king of Norway. Like Baldr, men had disquieting dreams before dying in battles, and as in the run-up to Ragnarøk, norms of behavior faded. For example, after an ambush at Örlýgsstaðir in 1238 that killed the chieftains Sturla Sighvatsson and his father, and fifty of their followers, several men took sanctuary in a nearby church. When their opponents threatened to burn the church and declared their asylum to be in-valid, they came out and were slain.

Probably the event that most echoed the fading of norms of proper behavior was an attack on the chieftain Gizurr Þorvaldsson at his home in Flugumýri in 1253. A principal of the battle of Örlýgsstaðir, he had tried to broker a peace and was to marry the daughter of his former enemy, Sturla Þórðarson (a nephew of Snorri Sturluson). A disgruntled opponent of the settlement and his followers set fire to the hall and burned to death men, women, and children. In this context, giving obedience to the Norwegian king a decade later might be seen as an action that avoided Ragnarøk. We can only spec-ulate about such connections, to be sure, but it is worth mentioning that Snorri Sturluson, himself a player in these struggles until he was murdered in 1244, gave his "booth" or temporary residence at the annual *alþingi* "general assembly," the perhaps ironic name Valhǫll. Furthermore, the Icelandic book of settlements (*Landnámabók*), whose lost antecedents go back to the twelfth century, has a little anecdote, supported by an anonymous *dróttkvætt* stanza, saying that when the sons of Hjalti Þórðarson, Þorvaldr and Þórðr, came to the *þing* "assembly" at Þorskafjörður after taking their inheritance from him, they were so well adorned that they looked like Æsir. This certainly shows that the old myths were good to think with.

Another indication that myths may have been good to think with is the "displacement" of mythic patterns from the divine world to the human world, that is, to the "historical" world of heroic legend. The clearest example would appear to be the figure of Hadingus, a legendary king who figures in the early books of Saxo's *Gesta Danorum*. Georges Dumézil (1987) has shown that Hadingus moves from a pattern of the Vanir, through an incestuous relationship with his mother, to that of the Æsir, through a relationship with Óðinn, and in this he is, in effect, a "displaced" version of the god Njǫrðr. There may also be displacement at work as well in the most famous Nordic hero, Sigurðr Fáfnisbani, who is descended from Óðinn: like Þórr, he kills a monster, and like Baldr, he dies at the hand of a close relative.[10]

The fourth and probably most important reason why the mythology should have survived as systematically as it appears to have done was its role, through the language of poetry, in preserving native wisdom, or to put it another way, lore that was encoded in native systems of memory, transmission, and performance. Both Sæmundr Sigfússon and Ari Þorgilsson bore the cognomen *fróði*, which is usually translated "learned" but more accurately perhaps should be translated "learned in native lore." Sæmundr's lost work dealt with the kings of Norway, and although Ari's *Íslendingabók* focuses on Icelandic ecclesiastical history, it is framed by royal history, and according to the *Prologue* an earlier version contained lives of kings. This is significant because the lives of kings were documented in the verse of their skalds, and that verse would have been unintelligible without comprehensive knowledge of myth and heroic legend

---

[10] Some scholars have argued the reverse, namely that Sigurðr was once a god or demigod. Personally I doubt this argument, but even if it holds, it still shows that the myths were good to think with.

in order to unravel the kennings. The most *fróðr* god in the mythology was Óðinn, and when in the eddic poem *Vafþrúðnismál* he
contests in *frœði* "wisdom" (a noun derived from the root *fróð-*) with
Vafþrúðnir, the wisest of giants, the subject is mythological knowledge. The conversion to Christianity made it illegal to worship the
old gods, but to lose the mythology in which they figured would
have been to lose the past.

If the myths were transmitted, at least sometimes, in the old
Germanic alliterative meter, it follows that poets and other *fróðir*
menn "wise people" would have continued to learn and transmit
poems very like the eddic poems that exist, and if the myths and
legends in them were fundamental to the memory of the past, it
follows that a systematizer, animated by something like what animated Snorri, but operating in a different mode, could have gathered
together such poems into what we now call the *Poetic Edda*. This
manuscript, first mentioned in the Introduction, is very carefully
organized. The first poem, *Vǫluspá*, which has figured frequently
in these pages as in all treatments of Old Norse mythology, offers a
synopsis of the mythology focusing on the beginning and the end. It
exists, as has been noted, in two different manuscript versions; the
one in the *Poetic Edda* is the one that includes the death of Baldr and
its apparent link to Ragnarøk. There follow poems in which Óðinn is
the protagonist: *Hávamál*, a conglomerate of several parts, including
Óðinn's self-sacrifice on the tree and acquisition of knowledge;
Vafþrúðnismál, the contest of wisdom with the giant Vafþrúðnir; and
Grímnismál, the ecstatic wisdom performance in the hall of King
Geirrøðr. Then comes *Skírnismál*, the story of Freyr's wooing of
the giantess Gerðr. Some observers have thought that the redactor
was following the order of their deaths at Ragnarøk, but it seems
just as likely to me that he prioritized the two gods from whom
kings descended, namely Óðinn and Freyr. A series of Þórr poems
follows: *Hárbarðsljóð*, the verbal duel between Óðinn and Þórr;
Hymiskviða, in which Þórr obtains the kettle for brewing beer and in
the course of acquiring it fishes up the world serpent; *Lokasenna*, in

which Loki tells home truths about the gods until Þórr silences him; and *Þrymskviða*, in which Þórr dresses up as Freyja to retrieve his stolen hammer from the giant Þrymr. The next poem, *Vǫlundarkviða* "The Poem of Volund," seems to us more a heroic legend than a myth, but the redactor apparently seized on the characterization of the protagonist as one of the *álfar*, a mythological group associated with the Æsir. The final poem, *Alvíssmál*, again features Þórr, but the redactor probably placed it here because Alvíss is a dwarf.

The rest of the manuscript contains poems recounting heroic legend, again organized with a synoptic poem at the beginning and grouping the following poems by protagonist. We recall Snorri's arrangement of kennings in *Skáldskaparmál*: gods, heroes, and Christ, and in that light it seems that the learned redactor of the *Poetic Edda* may have felt that the stories that followed on from the ones he had arranged so carefully were those of Christian history.

We owe these medieval intellectuals a debt of gratitude. Without them, it would have been impossible to say anything meaningful about Old Norse mythology.

Chapter 4

Old Norse Mythology and Ideology
(and Entertainment)

This chapter will show that Old Norse mythology has served ideological purposes in various ways almost as far back as we can see. Indeed, if the theories of Georges Dumézil hold, we see ideological structures deep into the Indo-European past. In an enormous body of writing that spanned half a century, Dumézil argued for the appearance of three "functions" in the mythologies of Indo-European peoples, and therefore that these functions were an inheritance of proto-Indo-European myth and religion. By "function" Dumézil meant something like the mythological realization of certain basic social principles, namely sovereignty, force, and fertility. Over time a kind of shorthand grew up, and these became known as the first, second, and third functions. Sovereignty, Dumézil thought, comprised two aspects: the awe inspired by the sovereign in his cosmic role, and the legal apparatus of society. Force, the second function, defended society, and fertility, the third function, enabled people, animals, and crops to prosper. Early in his career Dumézil argued that these functions were anchored to social classes (nobles, warriors, farmers), but later he abandoned this idea and treated the functions as ideological constructs.

Dumézil applied this theory explicitly to Old Norse mythology.[1] The awesome and cosmic side of the function of sovereignty, he argued, was filled by Óðinn, and the legal/juridical side by Týr. The function of force was filled by Þórr, and that of fertility by the Vanir. The fit of Óðinn with awesome rulership and the cosmos is good, that of Týr with legal matters less so: Dumézil argued this point on the basis of the binding of the wolf Fenrir, in which he sacrificed his hand to uphold an oath—but it was a false oath. The connection of Þórr with force is obvious, and indeed Þórr compares readily with other Indo-European "second-function" figures. Similarly, it is easy to see the Vanir as associated with fertility. Indeed, perhaps the major contribution of Dumézil's analysis of Old Norse mythology was to show convincingly that the war between the Æsir and Vanir was an ideological myth, not the reflection of an actual war between groups with different cult practices, as had been the prevailing view in the nineteenth and earlier twentieth centuries.

Dumézil's analysis was quite influential in the middle of the last century, but it was never without skeptics. For one thing, to study Indo-European is to study so many different languages and cultures that it requires prodigious learning, and sometimes Dumézil's work with details did not meet the expectations of specialists. And for some, the paradigm seemed too general—identical, indeed, with the medieval Christian division into priests and nobles, warriors, and farmers. Still, the theory is "good to think with," and even if one accepts only part or even none of it, it draws attention to the fact that myth and ideology go hand in hand.

As the influence of Dumézil has waned, scholars have come to accept there was a ruler ideology during the Viking Age, and probably before, that drew on the relationship between the ruler and

---

[1] Dumézil's scholarly output was enormous and sometimes repetitive. The most representative example of his treatment of Old Norse mythology in English is Dumézil 1973, which includes a translation of the 1959 revision of his 1939 original book on Old Norse mythology, along with several relevant articles.

the gods.[2] In *Ynglinga saga* ch. 8, Snorri wrote about the social contract with Óðinn, a human king taken to be a god by his followers in Sigtuna:

> In all Sweden men paid tribute to Óthin, a penny for every head; and he was to defend their land against incursions and to make sacrifice for them so that they would have good seasons. [Hollander 1964: 12]

Although Snorri is writing with a euhemeristic perspective, he gives a good indication of what rulership probably entailed during the Viking Age. The ruler had to function as a leader in war and a leader in peace, to ensure victory in battle and a sufficient food supply. In *Germania* ch. 7 Tacitus made a distinction between *reges* "kings" and *duces* "military leaders," implying that they were different persons. Those who study Germanic and early Scandinavian religion sometimes talk of "peace kings" and "war kings," although these should be regarded as conceptual categories rather than absolute social reality. It is believed that somewhere around the fifth century the importance of the "war king" increased along with the institution of the warrior band, a group of men whose purpose was mainly waging war, who were bound to a leader and whose lives were lived fully within the band rather than in normal household patterns. Such institutions had long existed, but they seem to have become more important in the centuries before the Viking Age, perhaps also in connection with a growth in the importance of rulers' halls. The ruler ideology within these warrior bands was presumably closely tied up with the mythology of Óðinn, especially in his role as successful military leader and ruler of the hall Valhǫll, where warriors who had fallen in battle on earth served as Óðinn's *einherjar*. They fought and feasted as they awaited the final battle at Ragnarøk, just

---

[2] For a recent survey of this subject, see Schjødt 2020.

as the members of the warrior elite enjoyed life in the chieftain's hall as they awaited the next battle.

However, it is important to bear in mind that the sources tell us that the object of cult activity was often *ár ok friðr* "good harvest and peace." Alongside the "war-king" ideology of Óðinn and the war bands there was surely something like a "peace-king" ideology, which is captured in the end of the earlier quotation about Óðinn. However, the main representative of this ideology is Freyr— not as we see him in the two *Eddas*, where he is a rather pale figure, who does, however, sacrifice his sword (emblem of a "war-king"?) for sexual lust (attribute of a "peace-king?), but rather in what we can glean about him in Sweden. In *Ynglinga saga*, Snorri wrote that Njǫrðr succeeded Óðinn and was in turn succeeded by Freyr. About Njǫrðr he says, in ch. 9: "In his days good peace prevailed and there were such good crops of all kinds that the Swedes believed that Njorth had power over the harvests and the prosperity of mankind" (Hollander 1964: 13). This reiteration of the euhemerism that characterizes *Ynglinga saga* is consistent with the ideology of the "peace-king," and that of Freyr is even more so. In ch. 10 we learn that Freyr constructed the great temple in Uppsala (i.e., carried out the cult functions of the ruler) and amassed the wealth of the crown (the means of fulfilling the duties of the ruler):

> In his days there originated the so-called Peace of Fróthi. There were good harvests at that time in all countries. The Swedes attributed that to Frey. And he was worshipped more than other gods because in his days, owing to peace and good harvests, the farmers became better off than before. [Hollander 1964: 13–14]

Snorri is again juxtaposing mythic history to world history. As we have seen, the peace of Fróði was a Nordic name (at least in the eyes of learned men like Snorri) for the Pax Augustana, the peace that took place when Christ was on earth. Still, even if he is not the cause of it, Freyr is rewarded by his subjects for bestowing peace and plenty on them—so much so, indeed, that after he died, according to this same chapter in *Ynglinga saga*, his followers put him in a mound with a door and windows and told the Swedes that he was still alive.[3] For three years they continued offering tribute, which they flung through the windows into the mound, and for these three years peace and plenty continued.[4]

Although it was recorded in the thirteenth century in a euhemeristic frame, the story of Freyr in the mound reflects much of the ruler ideology of Old Norse mythology. There is in effect a contract between the ruler and the people: the ruler presides over cult and through his contact with the gods provides peace and plenty. Furthermore, the euhemeristic frame makes it easy to see another aspect of this ruler ideology: a human king could be worshipped after his death. Indeed:

> When all Swedes knew that Frey was dead but that good seasons and peace still prevailed, they believed this would be the case so long as Frey was in Sweden; and so they would not burn him and called him the God of the World and sacrificed to him ever after for good harvests and peace. [Hollander 1964: 14]

Here it is important to recall that the boundary between gods and humans was far less clear-cut than it is in the world religions with which we are familiar today, as I mentioned in the Introduction. If rulers could become gods, it enhanced their status in life and in death, and it also helped their subjects feel confident that their own

---

[3] This way of putting it emphasizes that Freyr was one of Óðinn's followers, who had immigrated from Asia, according to the euhemeristic frame. Thus, like the crafty Æsir from Troy in *Gylfaginning*, they deceive the Swedes.

[4] In *Gesta Danorum* V, 16, Saxo tells a similar story about the Danish king Frotho (=Fróði), who is conceptually very like Freyr and may once have been identical to him. The motivation of Frotho's followers is to some degree to preserve the peace, since they fear revolt at the news of the king's death and wish to discourage any invasion that might follow on the news.

needs were known to the gods. Some recensions of the *Saga of St
Óláfr* tell of a prehistoric Norwegian king from Geirstad in southern
Norway, also named Óláfr, who specifically warned his followers not
to worship him after his death. They did so anyway. Thereafter he
gained the cognomen Geirstaðaálfr "*álfr* of Geirstad." Although this
little story is part of the learned literature about Norway's saint and
rex perpetuus "permanent king," it shows that ideas of the worship of
kings after their deaths were plausible in medieval Scandinavia, no
doubt because they had always been so.

Another aspect of ruler ideology was the descent of kings from
the gods. The royal line known as the Ynglingar were said to descend from Yngvi, which the learned men who recorded the mythology tell us was another name for Freyr (indeed, sometimes he
is called Yngvi-Freyr). Freyr was particularly attached to the Svear,
the people who lived in the area around Lake Mälar in Sweden, with
Uppsala the most important central place. Descent from the gods
was a qualification for rulership, as was proper carrying out of the
cult. "Together with some ritual actions performed during the in-
vestiture, the mythical background provided the ruler with the necessary qualities for and rights to rulership" (Sundqvist 2002: 367).

Elsewhere in Scandinavia, the jarls of Lade traced their descent
to a union between Óðinn and Skaði. Hákon jarl Sigurðarson figures
in the written sources as a virulent pagan and the most powerful opponent of the conversion to Christianity in Norway. And Hákon and
the other Lade jarls were not the only rulers to claim descent from
Óðinn; even some royal houses in England claimed Wodæn as an
ancestor. Descent from the gods was clearly a powerful component
of ruler ideology.

The prose frame of the eddic poem *Grímnismál* suggests a possible role of the gods in royal succession. According to the prose
header, two kings' sons are shipwrecked on an island where they are
fostered by an old couple (Óðinn and Frigg). Óðinn gets a boat for
them but secretly advises one, Geirrøðr, to push the other back out
to sea when they reach home. The old king has died, and Geirrøðr is
taken as king, and it is this Geirrøðr whom Óðinn visits to investigate

Frigg's claim, made in the prose header, that Geirrøðr is stingy with food. The prose header also says that Frigg has sent a minion to warn Geirrøðr that his impending visitor has dangerous magical powers, and that is why Geirrøðr suspends Óðinn over the fire, where he has his ecstatic wisdom performance. The poem itself ends with the epiphany of Óðinn, but then the story goes on in prose:

> Geirrod the king sat with a sword on his lap, half drawn from the sheath. But when he heard that it was Odin who had come there, he stood up and intended to pull Odin away from the fire. The sword slipped from his hand, hilt downwards. The king lost his footing and plunged forwards, and the sword pierced him through, and he was killed. Odin disappeared. And Agnar was then king for a long time afterwards. [Larrington 2014: 56]

This myth suggests that Óðinn was actively involved in choosing the moment of succession within rulership, first by advising Geirrøðr how to get rid of his brother, second by causing Geirrøðr to die so that his son Agnarr can succeed him. Taken more broadly, this myth suggests that the gods were involved in choosing rulers, or to put it another way, that rulers ruled because the gods had chosen them.

The "learned prehistory" and the associated euhemerism of Snorri Sturluson and Saxo Grammaticus also, of course, represented attempts to situate the mythology within a discourse of ideology, specifically to create a deep history tying the ruling elites to Asia Minor, the center of the Christian world in the Middle Ages. Instead of being pagan gods or demons (which were the same in the eyes of the Church), or ancestors living in mounds, the gods of the mythology were flesh-and-blood humans who established the predecessors of some of the social institutions in place, the others having been brought by the Church. And by the same token, the demonization of the old gods fit and supported the ideology of the Church. The old gods actually do seem to have lived on, at least in name, in magical charms (Mitchell 2020), but they are in effect demons called upon to work magic outside the operations of God and the Church.

A Norwegian charm intended to disclose the identity of a thief, incised in runes, shows this clearly: "I exhort you, Óðinn, with heathendom, the greatest of fiends" (Mitchell 2011: 12). This exhortation calls upon an aspect of Óðinn that we can infer from the mythology, namely that he knows the location of hidden valuables; Snorri wrote in *Ynglinga saga* ch. 7 that Óðinn knew all about where buried treasure was concealed and could go into the earth and get it. So a charm like this medieval runic inscription may well represent the mythology reconfigured in light of the dominant ideology.

Much later, and down into the nineteenth and early twentieth centuries, folk legends circulated about "Odin's hunt," a version of the legend of the Wild Hunt, in which a group of spirits rushes through the sky following a demonic leader (figure 4.1 offers a

FIGURE 4.1 Peter Nicolai Arbo, *Åsgårdsreien*, oil on canvas, 1872. In this depiction of the "ride of Ásgarðr," a wild hunter (Óðinn) on an eight-legged black horse leads the riders; Þórr can be glimpsed among the riders, holding his hammer aloft. Some of the riders snatch up innocent passers-by to join them. Photo © O. Vaering/Bridgeman Images.

romantic depiction of the legend). The leader is often said to have been condemned to hunt supernatural beings forever as punishment for having hunted on a Sunday. Some scholars have argued that Óðinn has always properly belonged to the Wild Hunt, which would combine his connections with the dead and warrior band, but even if that is so, the folk legends have been adapted to Christian ideology.

Legends often reinforce norms of behavior, and to the legends of Odin's hunt may be compared legends in which a hunter is out on Sunday and overhears trolls planning to capture and eat him. He rushes back to church.

As the Middle Ages drew to a close, the ancient gods were duly described—briefly—by historians such as Albert Krantz and the Uppsala bishops Johannes Magnus and Olaus Magnus. They followed Adam of Bremen, who wrote in his *History of the Archbishops of Hamburg Bremen* (c. 1070) that the pagan temple at Uppsala had idols of Þórr (the head deity according to Adam), Óðinn, and Freyr. Interestingly, the sixteenth-century historians understood Adam's Fricco (=Freyr) to refer to Freyja, and thus she replaces Freyr in their accounts, as in figure 4.2.

They euhemerize the old gods following Saxo.

A far more accurate description of the mythology was offered by the Icelander Arngrímur Jónsson in his *Crymogæa sive rerum Islandarum* "'Ice-land' or Matters Icelandic" (1609). Arngrímur's treatise was inspired by patriotism; he sought to counter the prevailing image of Iceland as a barbaric land on the outer edge of civilization. Rather, he wrote, it had a vigorous literary tradition, of which the mythology represented an important aspect. Arngrímur was the first author to use the mythology in an ideology of patriotism, and as one of the first humanist scholars to reconnect with the medieval Icelandic manuscript tradition, he enabled other such patriotic engagements.

The seventeenth century saw the emergence of Denmark and Sweden on the world stage as great powers. Denmark had a far-flung

DE SVPERSTITIO. CVL. DAEMO.

De tribus Diis maioribus Gothorum.

FIGURE 4.2 Woodcut from Olaus Magnus, *Historia de Gentibus Septentrionalis* (Rome, 1555), 3, 3–4, showing the gods of the ancient "Goths." From left are "Frigga, Thor, Odhen." This illustration also appeared in Johannes Magnus's *Historia de omnibus Gothorum Suenumque regibus* (Rome, 1554). Some of the details of the image of Þórr appear to follow Hans Holbein the Younger's illustrations for 1 Chronicles 9:1 (Granlund 1976: 354). Project Runeberg (public domain).

empire encompassing not just Norway but also parts of present-day southern Sweden, which give Denmark full control over access to the Baltic, as well as, for most of the period, the Baltic islands of Bornholm, Gotland, and Ösel, and the Atlantic colonies in the Faroes, Iceland, and Greenland; indeed, Denmark even had trading footholds in Africa and India. Sweden, however, was the really great northern power from 1632 until the death of the young king Karl XII in 1718. At its height, Sweden controlled not only Finland, as it had since the Viking Age, but also Ingria, Estonia, and Livonia along the Baltic, and it gained military victories in Poland and elsewhere. Great powers need great national pasts, and the Icelandic scholars who had come to the Scandinavian cities and universities as humanism took hold had the key to a vast repository of the Nordic past, namely Old Norse literature, most of which had been recorded and was being rediscovered in Iceland.

During the age of great military power (1632–1718), Sweden found a scholar who expounded its previous greatness and indeed, its primacy among nations, in the Uppsala professor Olof Rudbeck (the elder). Discover of the lymphatic system and dedicated anti-quarian, he devoted the later part of his career to proving not only that Sweden had been Atlantis the lost continent, but also the cradle of humanity and civilization. In a remarkable series of four volumes bearing the main title *Atlantica* (1679–1702—the year of his death), Rudbeck drew on an astonishing wealth of sources to support his theories. Old Norse mythology was just one of these sources. In the first instance,[5] Rudbeck thought that that the word the Greeks used for persons who dwelt in the North, *hyperborean* "beyond Boreas" (i.e., the North wind), contained the name of Búri (whom he knew as Bore), the forefather of the Æsir, who would rule the heavens and the earth, and this inspired him to think of glorious prehistoric Swedish kings. The gods of Old Norse mythology, he later claimed, were the originals of the Greek gods: Apollo was actually Baldr, Zeus was actually Þórr, Neptune was actually Njǫrðr, and Hades was actually Óðinn (see King 2005: 166–72). While Rudbeck's theories had multiple admirers and adherents in Sweden, they gained little traction outside and were beginning to fade even before the death of the warrior king Karl XII in 1718.

Translations of *Heimskringla* were published in Copenhagen in 1633 and in Stockholm in 1697, thus bringing Snorri's brief and euhemerized version of the mythology in the early chapters of *Ynglinga* saga before the public eye. In 1665 Peder Hansen Resen, a professor at the University of Copenhagen, published *Edda Islandorum* "the Edda of the Icelanders," that is, Snorri's *Edda*, and editions of *Vǫluspá* and *Hávamál*. The *Edda* was based on a

---

[5] This example is taken from King 2005: 72–75.

postmedieval re-arrangement of one manuscript by the Icelandic priest Magnús Ólafsson undertaken early in the seventeenth century and sometimes now known as the Laufás *Edda* for the farm where he later had a living. Magnús broke the text into two parts:[6] narratives (Icelandic *dæmisögur* "exempla") and kennings, which he listed alphabetically by referent, from *Æsir* "gods" to *þang* "seaweed." Because this version of Snorri's *Edda* was better known in early modern Iceland than the medieval manuscripts of the text, it was natural that Resen should choose it. The text he printed was trilingual: alongside the Old Norse are Latin and Danish translations.

A partial edition and translation of a medieval manuscript of Snorri's *Edda*, the one in the Uppsala University Library, was issued in Sweden in 1746 by the antiquarian Johan Göransson, accompanied by Swedish and Latin translations. He followed this with an edition and Swedish translation of *Vǫluspá* in 1750. That Göransson subscribed to the theories that had been put forth by Rudbeck is shown by the title, the first half of which runs as follows: *De yfverborna atlingars, eller, sviogötars ok nordmänners, Edda, det är, stammodren för deras, uti hedendomen, både andliga ok verldsliga vishet* . . . "The Edda of the descendants of the Yfirborna, or the Sviogötar or Northmen, that is, the ancestral mother, within paganism, of their spiritual and worldly wisdom. . ." These were large claims to make for a small book, but they were hitched to the enormous movement that Rudbeck had started.

Sporadic translations occurred from time to time thereafter, but Old Norse mythology received international attention when, in 1755 and 1756, Paul Henri Mallet, a Swiss-born professor at the University of Copenhagen, published *Introduction à l'histoire de Dannemarc ou l'on traite de la religion, des mœurs, des lois, et des usages des anciens Danois* "Introduction to the history of Denmark in which are treated the religion, customs, laws, and practices of the old Danes" and

---

[6] Because Icelanders have patronymics ("son of") or occasionally matronymics ("daughter of") rather than surnames, it is customary to refer to them by their given names.

Monumens de la mythologie et de la poésie des Celtes et particulièrement des anciens Scandinaves "Monuments of the mythology and poetry of the Celts and especially of the old Scandinavians." The first volume is in fact given over entirely to an "introduction" to the subject of Danish history, and the second to translated narratives of the Laufás *Edda* into French (from the Latin translations rather than the Old Norse). The first, however, has considerable treatment of the old myth and religion. Immediately following, in Book 3, are claims that the ancient Scandinavians lived in an orderly political system built on liberty and freedom, in which kings consulted their councils and decisions were undertaken more or less jointly. This was certainly in the spirit of the Enlightenment, even if the Danish monarchy was still absolute.[7] The work is dedicated to the king (Christian VI), who had commissioned the work, with a flattering presentation of the nature of the monarchy in Denmark (for a detailed analysis of the impact of this work, see Zernack 2018).

By "Celtic" Mallet meant the indigenous, non-classical religions "of the Gauls and of Brittany, of Germania and Scandinavia, of the vast expanses of Scythia" (vol. 2, 6, my translation), and he believed that Old Norse mythology reflected all of them. When Thomas Percy published his influential English revised and adapted translation of Mallet in 1770, *Northern Antiquities*, he included a "Translator's Preface" devoted mostly to showing that Celtic and Germanic were separate language families, thus removing the unfortunate designation "Celtic" for Old Norse mythology. A result of this linguistic classification, of course, was to suggest that the mythology of Snorri's *Edda*, couched as it was in one Germanic language, was also presumably the mythology of the English, who spoke another Germanic language. This is something we still believe today.

If Percy's *Reliques of Ancient Poetry* (1765) was more influential than the translation of Mallet in ushering in the era of romantic

---

[7] In Sweden, by contrast, the period 1719–1766 is known as the Age of Liberty.

poetry in English, we must not forget adaptations/translations such as Thomas Grey's Norse odes from 1768 ("The Fatal Sisters" and "Odin's Descent to Hel") and other similar verse. Notwithstanding a certain amount of poetry inspired by the mythology (O'Donoghue 2014), in nineteenth-century England the sagas came to replace the myths as the focus of interest (Wawn 2000: 32).

Mallet's was not the only major contribution to the study of Old Norse mythology in eighteenth-century Denmark. The Icelandic-born Árni Magnússon, a professor and state functionary in Copenhagen, had collected many Icelandic manuscripts (among them the fragmentary manuscript of eddic mythological poetry), and upon his death in 1730 he bequeathed this collection to the university. Over the years it was augmented. In the year 1778 a group of Icelandic scholars working under the auspices of the will began publication of an edition of the mythological poems of the *Poetic Edda* (*Edda Sæmundar hinns fróda* 1778–1828), leaving out, however, the poems that Resen had published, namely *Vǫluspá* and *Hávamál*.[8] A forty-eight-page state of the (late eighteenth-century) art introduction, facing Latin translations, and extensive notes to the texts meant that anyone who knew Latin (that is, anyone who was educated) now had access to the heart of the mythological corpus, both the mythological eddic poems and the mythological narratives of Snorri's *Edda*. A later second volume covered the heroic poems, and a final third volume (1828) contained the missing *Vǫluspá* and *Hávamál*, as well as *Rígsþula* "The List of Rig," but was mostly filled by a 600-page "Lexicon Mythologicum," an alphabetical listing of characters and concepts within the mythology compiled by Finnur Magnússon, thus giving the learned world a kind of handbook of the mythology.

The young Adam Oehlenschläger's 1803 poem "*Guldhornerne*" (The golden horns) ushered romanticism into Denmark and

---

[8] Their names do not appear on the 1787 title page, but we know them to have been Guðmundur Magnússon, Jón Jónsson, Jón Ólafsson, Finnur Magnússon, and Gunnar Pálsson.

Scandinavia. It has been said that Oehlenschläger's enthusiasm for the Nordic past was kindled by a class he took in high school on Old Norse mythology (Gosse 1911).[9] The golden horns themselves, early Iron Age artifacts with images and a runic inscription, had just been stolen (and were melted down), and Oehlenschläger used them as a symbol of Denmark's glorious Nordic past (see replicas of the horns in figure 4.3).

In subsequent works he drew on Old Norse mythology, as in the epic poem *Thors reise til Jotunheim* "Þórr's journey to Giantland" and the drama *Baldur hin gode* "Baldr the good," as well as on the sagas. Directly inspired by Oehlenschläger's verse,[10] Rasmus Nyerup issued a partial translation of Snorri's *Edda* into Danish (1808). In the same year N. F. S Grundtvig, the philosopher, theologian, and hymnist, then still early in his career, published a presentation of Old Norse mythology "for educated people who are not expert in mythology" (Grundtvig 1808), so that was a busy year for Old Norse mythology in Denmark. Grundtvig refined his theological and philosophical views and in 1832 published a new treatment incorporating these views. Oehlenschläger, too, offered a reorganization of the mythology in his epic *Nordens guder* (1819). In stanzas of eight lines with stress and rhyme patterns reminiscent of ballads, Oehlenschläger gives Þórr preference, opening with the journey to Útgarðaloki and coming finally to the theft and recovery of his hammer. In between, many of the myths are recast, although the role of Óðinn is quite attenuated. The epic turns the structure of the *Poetic Edda* around, ending with the prophecy of the seeress that is

---

[9] In this context may be mentioned the dictionary-like handbook of Jacob Bærent Møinichen treating "superstition, gods, fables, and heroes" (Møinichen 1801). In actual fact the entries are mostly names taken from the mythology, from Saxo, and from ballads. The spirit behind this work seems to be essentially historic: thus rather than try to bring together different presentations of Óðinn in the sources, Møinichen simply has entries on three figures named Odin.

[10] In the preface, Nyerup addresses the actor Stephan Heger (who played in a number of Oehlenschläger's dramas), saying that he is meeting Heger's desire that the public be able to understand properly Oehlenschläger's verse.

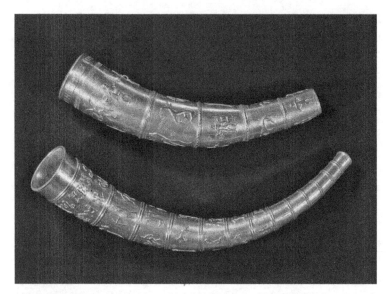

FIGURE 4.3   Replicas of the golden horns from Gallehus, Jylland, Denmark. The originals, usually dated from the early fifth century, were stolen and melted down in 1802. The figures on the horns have not been convincingly interpreted, but the runic inscription on the upper horn identifies the maker of the horn (text and translation are in this book's Introduction). Lennart Larsen, Nationalmuseet, Denmark.

the subject of *Vǫluspá* at the beginning of the *Poetic Edda*. At the end of the epic, Oehlenschläger's seeress sings in prophecy the demise of the gods but then consoles them with a vision of joy and happiness. Oehlenschläger thus puts a very personal stamp on the mythology, as literary artists have continued to do.

   In Sweden the national romantic spirit was institutionalized in an organization, founded in 1811, that called itself Götiska förbundet ("the Gothic league"). "Gothic" was the term that Rudbeck had used for the old Swedes who lived in the cradle of civilization,[11] and

---

[11] The following lines are based on the summary of the organization provided by von Friesen 1883.

the league that took it up in the early nineteenth century consisted originally of eleven patriotic young men in Stockholm who met to discuss antiquity, not least mythology (and to drink). They took on Old Norse names within the society, rarely from the gods, although one member who joined later took the rather pessimistic name Baldur. According to the statutes of the organization, its goals included reviving "the spirit of freedom, manly courage, and honest heart of the old 'Goths,' " and the love of each "Goth" for his native country was to be unfeigned, "his noblest deed to sacrifice life and blood for its independence." Here patriotism and antiquarianism recognize Sweden's loss of Finland to Russia in 1807 and the implicit threat of Russian military might, as well as the governmental reform of 1809. The society published a journal at irregular intervals, containing some now famous romantic poems as well as articles on antiquarian subjects. The name of the journal was taken from Old Norse mythology: *Iduna*, a Latinized form of the goddess Iðunn. Outside the confines of the journal, one of the founding members, the poet P. H. Ling, published a presentation of the mythology's "symbolic system [*sinnebildslära*], for the unlearned" in 1819, which begins with a preface explaining the idea of national character and extolling the Nordic. This will have come in handy for those who had read the Swedish translation of the *Poetic Edda* issued in the previous year by A. A. Afzelius (1818) with no explanatory matter except a brief preface about the persons upon whose work he had built; the preface was in Latin, so one presumes that the unlearned could make little use of it. The year 1819 also saw a new translation of parts of Snorri's *Edda* into Swedish (Cnattingius 1819). If the epicenter of Old Norse mythology was a decade earlier in Denmark than in Sweden, that was typical of the way cultural trends moved between the two nations.

Norway left Denmark in 1814 for a loose union with Sweden that would last until 1907. As the new nation sought to find its identity, the folklore of the rural countryside came to play a far greater role than it did in Denmark or Sweden. Perhaps as a result, Old Norse mythology played a smaller ideological role, although of course the results of the Danish fascination with Old Norse mythology were readily available to the reading in public in Norway, since Danish had been the literary language for centuries; the distinctive forms of Norwegian (there are two) were formulated only later in the nineteenth century. As far as I can tell, the first translation of the *Poetic Edda* to be published in Norway was that of Gjessing in 1866, by which time the academic discipline of Old Norse studies had been flourishing for some while. Gjessing based his translation on Sophus Bugge's still usable edition, and the language is quite conservative.

Mallet was translated into German in 1776. Herder, the father of national romanticism, had included a translation of *Vǫluspá* in his enormously influential *Volkslieder* "Folk songs" (1778–1779), and Old Norse mythology figured fairly prominently thereafter. Friedrich David Gräter published a book called *Nordische Blumen* "Nordic flowers" in 1789, which contained translations of a mix of materials, including several eddic mythological poems. In 1791 Gräter teamed with Gottfried Böckh to put out a journal called *Bragur, ein literarisches Magazin der deutschen und nordischen Vorzeit* "Bragur, a literary magazine for German and Nordic antiquity." *Bragur* (Old Norse *bragr*) means "poetry," and the "poetry" that the editors found for the first volume was all from Old Norse. In later numbers Gräter found room (as sole editor after the death of Böckh) for English and German subjects, but Old Norse still predominated. Thus, because of the linguistic affinity (and the lack of any significant mythological material in German), Old Norse mythology became a vehicle for advancing ideas about the German people. Indeed, the first major scholarly work on the subject, by Jacob Grimm (1835), bore the title *Deutsche Mythologie* "German mythology."

Bragur (later also called *Braga und Hermode*) ceased publication in 1812, and in 1812 Gräter started a second journal, this one called *Idunna und Hermode* (that is, Iðunn and Hermóðr). The contents were quite a mixed bag, but the overall Nordic orientation could be seen literally on the title page, where the main title was spelled out in runes. Underneath it stood the subtitle: *Eine Altertumszeitung* "A journal of antiquity." In the second number in 1812, the Brothers Grimm announced their plan for a translation of the *Poetic Edda* (Grimm and Grimm 1815—actually, it was just the heroic poems). That was also the year in which they began publication of their fairy tale collection (Grimm and Grimm 1812–1815).

Another strand in German nationalism also was emergent at around this time. Friedrich Rühs, who issued a book on the mythology in 1812, including a translation of Snorri's *Edda*, also was among those who wrote of the threat posed by Jews, especially to the "Germanic world" (see Rühs 1815 for a polemical anti-Semitic pamphlet).

With this we open a sad chapter in the relationship between Old Norse mythology and ideology. Even if it supported imperialist agendas, the yoking of mythology to the nation state in the early modern North and the post-enlightenment discovery of a people in its "antiquities," these pale before the hijacking of the mythology by anti-Semites in nineteenth-century Germany and by the Nazis, and down to this day by white supremacists in North American and northern Europe. Richard Wagner's sublime Ring cycle is a pinnacle of musical and dramatic achievement, with the humanized world of the gods giving way to the inexorable move, driven by human emotions, toward the end, and the subsequent renewal that is sounded by the final bars. While it is possible to read the Nibelungen, or Alberich, the dwarf who renounces love and thus takes down the cosmos, as Wagner's twisted projection of Jews, there is nothing whatever in the mythology to justify such a projection. That was Wagner's understanding of what makes a people, a distortion of the romantics' ideas in that it leaves out the universalist agenda that motivated the romantics alongside the national and is exclusive rather than inclusive.

Nor is there anything within the mythology itself, other than its partial derivation from (or passing through) Iron Age Germanic culture, to account for its attraction to Hitler and other leaders of

Nazi Germany, or today's white supremacists. Rather it is a mistaken idea of "Germanic purity," which can be "recovered from" the mythology only when one knows little or nothing of the multiple cultural contexts that helped form it, the circumstances of its actual use, and of the textual traditions that have come down to us. Stephanie von Schnurbein, who has studied Germanic neo-paganism extensively (von Schnurbein 1992, 1993, 2016, 2018), writes that in recent decades the relationship with purity has become rather complex. She sees three main variations within the literally dozens of usually small groups of "Asatruers" (a name often used for Germanic neopagans, based on Icelandic *ásatrú* "belief in the Æsir"). The first two, "racial-religious," and "ethnicist," seek purity in race and culture, respectively. The third group, however, which von Schnurbein calls "a-racial," rejects the category of race and takes a more dynamic view of culture (von Schnurbein 2018: 491).

Obviously Old Norse mythology constitutes the textual basis of Germanic neopaganism, despite the fact that the corpus, as we have seen, was not recorded during the pre-Christian period and presents numerous interpretive challenges. As von Schnurbein writes, this fact is honored, but mostly in the breach:

> Today, the claim to know primary sources, as well as academic theory, plays a foundational role for the self-understanding and self-justification of a-racist and many ethnicist Asatruers. Yet the majority of these Heathens have little first-hand knowledge of these sources and the Old Norse or Latin languages that they are written in. Their knowledge comes mostly from fictional literature, Neopagan popular interpretations and other popularized accounts of Norse mythology, as well as from Internet sources. [von Schnurbein 2018: 515]

An exception to this statement would be the Ásatrúarfélag "ásatrú foundation" of Iceland, since Icelanders can read their medieval texts with relatively little difficulty. Perhaps this explains in part why ásatrú has been a recognized organized religion in Iceland since 1973 with plans very near fruition to build a temple on a Reykjavík hillside.[12]

Wagner's Ring cycle ends with—and everything before it points up to—*Götterdämmerung* "twilight of the gods." This is the same focus on end matters that in fact drives both *Vǫluspá* and Snorri's *Gylfaginning*, that presumably made sense to medieval Christians, and definitely made sense to Christians in later Europe, such as Grundtvig. Ragnarøk attracted two formidable writers to retell it in ways that embody their own ideological concerns of recent times. The first of these was the Danish author, philosopher, and critic Villy Sørensen (1929–2001). In 1978 he was one of three authors of the polemical book *Oprør fra midten* "Revolt from the center" (Meyer et al. 1978), which argued the feasibility of a middle way between communism and capitalism, taking features from each. When Sørensen set about to recast Old Norse mythology, he showed the same distaste for binaries and willingness to explore middle grounds. In his *Ragnarøk* (1988), the gods are all conflicted; relations between gods and giants are complex and individual; motivations are murky. Perhaps not surprisingly, the central figure is not Óðinn but Loki. As love and power face off against one another, the world of the gods becomes an increasingly untenable place, and finally Ragnarøk is inevitable. Written in a beguilingly simple style, the book teases out the complexities inherent in the mythology. Most interestingly, Sørensen omits the rebirth of the cosmos to be found in the sources, apparently taking it for an adaptation from Christianity. Be that as it may, Sorensen's *Ragnarok* was a Ragnarøk for its time. Villy Sørensen had come of age when fears of catastrophic nuclear destruction of the planet were all too real, and the anti-Soviet rhetoric of US President Ronald Reagan during the 1980s could certainly have revived such fears in a small NATO nation—and beyond. Sørensen's *Ragnarok* was translated into many languages including English.

---

[12] See the architect's website at http://magnus.jensson.is/?page_id=141.

If Sørensen gave the world a Ragnarøk for the Cold War, the novelist A. S. Byatt has done the same for our era. We have learned that even if we do not blow ourselves up and the planet with us, we have found other ways of destruction: the extinction of species, the reduction of biological complexity, the poisoning of the earth, sea, and sky. Byatt's Ragnarøk is told from the perspective of a young girl and her mother who move out into the English countryside for safety during World War II ("Nevertheless, by a paradoxical fate, the child may only have lived because her people left the sulphurous air of a steel city, full of smoking chimneys, for a country town, of no interest to enemy bombers" [Byatt 2011: 3].) This little girl, "the thin child," discovers a book of Norse mythology (Wägner 1880),[13] and from it the myths unfold along with the simple observations of the child and her interactions with the abundant nature around her, which seems boundless and endless; she picks wild flowers certain in the conviction that: "They flourished and faded and died and always came back next spring, and always would, the thin child thought, long after she herself was dead" (Byatt 2011: 35–36).

We must assume that all the mythic narratives are filtered through the consciousness and memory of the thin child, and sometimes, indeed, we are given her thoughts on a given myth or mythic detail.

Sometimes Byatt tells the myths sparsely, sometimes not. She lingers over the details of Ragnarøk, as for example in the onset of *fimbulvetr*, the terrible years of winter with no summer:

It began slowly. There were flurries of sharp snow over the fields where the oats and barley were ready to be harvested. There was ice on the dewponds at night, when the harvest moon, huge and red, was still in the sky. There was ice on water jugs and an increasing

---

[13] Byatt carries over from this work the idea that Jörmungandr, the World Serpent, is female, and offers a fascinating description of the growth of this monster and its interaction with Loki.

thin, bitter wind that did not let up, so that they became used to keeping their heads hooded and down. [Byatt 2011: 131]

Like Sørensen, the thin child stops the story here, although she knows that it goes on in her book. "She had stored Ragnarök against the time when it would become clear that her father would not come back" (Byatt 2011: 148). He does, however, and they move back to the "steel city," where her mother languishes from "dailiness" and nature loses its immediateness for her. At the end of the book, her father chops down an ash tree that grew wild in their garden, an innocent Yggdrasill.

In an afterword, "Thoughts on Myths," Byatt explains her narrative strategy, how the "thin child in wartime" built up a myth to cope with wartime: "Even if—indeed when—she herself came to an end the earth would go on renewing itself" (Byatt 2011: 166):

> But if you write a version of Ragnarök in the twenty-first century, it is haunted by the imagining of a different end of things. We are a species of animal which is bringing about the end of the world we were born into. Not out of evil or malice, or not mainly, but because of a lopsided mixture of extraordinary cleverness, extraordinary greed, extraordinary proliferation of our own kind, and a biologically built-in short-sightedness. [Byatt 2011: 167]

In an amusing reaction to new "gods" in contemporary life, such as The Technical Boy (the internet), Media, or The Intangibles (the "invisible hand" of the stock market), Neil Gaiman has a glass-eyed "Mr. Wednesday," that is, Óðinn, lead a gang of discarded gods of American immigrant and indigenous groups against these new gods. Although *American Gods* (2001) features old gods from a variety of traditions, the overriding plot is derived from Old Norse mythology: the protagonist, Shadow, reflects Baldr, whom Mr. Wednesday and Low Key Lyesmith (Loki) have manipulated in order to set up a new and chaotic Ragnarøk, which Shadow manages to avert. Recently (2017), Gaiman has issued a novelistic retelling of the mythology itself.

FIGURE 4.4 Þórr hooks the World Serpent in *Ormen i dybet* "The serpent in the depths" (Madsen et al. 1991), an album in the series Valhalla. The speakers are Heimdallr ("whom we brought along on the trip to Hymir" [Henning Kure, personal communication]) and Týr. Far-seeing Heimdallr (the figure above) reports the action far out at sea to Týr (the figure below): the serpent is bigger than Heimdallr thought, but Þórr fights with it anyway. "Naturally," replies Týr, "He's Þórr." Copyright © 2010 Peter Madsen et al.

The ideological use of the mythology is also to be found in pop culture. *The Mighty Thor* comic book series, launched in 1962, was in the first instance, as Martin Arnold has shown, a reaction to 1950s America, in which the comic book industry was forced to practice vigorous self-censorship. "Prurient images, profanities, graphic violence and anything that in any way whatsoever might cause offence to the most upright of citizens was banned" (Arnold 2011: 154–55). The comic-book character was a super-hero with a human alter-ego, great strength, and a willingness to defend the status quo, even if it changes; for example, Arnold amusingly points out the comic book Þórr's criticism of "slothful hippies" during the late 1960s and more seriously underlines the obvious truth: "*The Mighty Thor* has less to do with Norse myth and more to do with reflecting US political identity and the mood and mentality of contemporary US life, particularly as it might be perceived by comic-book consumers" (Arnold 2011: 158). Deleting references to the United States and to the specific medium, this sentence will serve as an apt judgment for all the materials adduced in this chapter.

As one final example we can take the wonderful Danish cartoon series *Valhalla* (1979–2009), drawn by Peter Madsen and scripted by the editor Henning Kure (who developed into an expert on Old Norse mythology and contributes regularly to the scholarly discussion of the subject [e.g., Kure 2010]), along with other writers, including Madsen (see figure 4.4).[14] This series hews far more closely than any other pop culture artifact to the actual Old Norse texts, with humorous changes or additions, sometimes in plot, sometimes added, slyly or not, in the illustrations.

The comics are, quite simply, really funny, but the underlying messages are those of Danish society: respect for others, equality of the sexes, equal pay for equal work, and so forth (see the treatment in Jón Karl Helgason 2017: 32–45).

---

[14]   For a thorough discussion of this series, see Hafner 2008.

Conclusion

Sacred Narrative?

As was noted in the Introduction, we probably come closest to the actual wording of sacred narratives in the *dróttkvætt* poems on mythological subjects that have been recorded in manuscripts of *Skáldskaparmál* in Snorri Sturluson's *Edda*. In chapter 2 we surveyed the material relating to Þórr's fishing expedition, and thus we have actually seen a great deal of the extant mythological *dróttkvætt* poetry, since the number of surviving longer poems is quite restricted, and nearly all the fragments relate to the fishing expedition. Only two other longer poems exist: Eilífr Goðrúnarson's *Þórsdrápa* "Þórr's (formal) poem" and Þjóðólfr ór Hvíni's *Haustlǫng* "Autumn-long." The relevant subjects were summarized briefly in chapter 1: *Þórsdrápa* treats Þórr's journey to and encounter with Geirrøðr and his daughters, and *Haustlǫng* as we have it now contains the stories of the loss and recovery of Iðunn, along with Þórr's duel with Hrungnir. Thus it is fair to say that in this form of narrative, myths of Þórr predominate. Although Óðinn appears in *Haustlǫng*'s story of Iðunn, the prime mover is Loki. Since we also have one stanza about a battle between Loki and Heimdallr in Úlfr Uggason's *Húsdrápa*, Loki figures more prominently than might be expected, and his role is certainly ambiguous: he both causes and solves the issue of the loss of Iðunn, and in fighting with Heimdallr he fights with a known god. If we add to this mix the other major story in *Húsdrápa*, namely the funeral of Baldr, we may well wonder about the absence of the other gods, especially Óðinn, but also Freyr, from whom kings descended (both Óðinn and Freyr do appear in Húsdrápa in the procession to Baldr's funeral), and Týr and Frigg, who gave their names to the days of the week. Even when we remind ourselves that the longer *dróttkvætt* poems are mostly descriptions of images on objects, and that Þórr's fishing expedition was the myth most widely found in images, the disparity seems strange. When we add to it the association of Óðinn and poetry within the mythology, it seems even stranger.

The picture becomes a bit clearer, however, when we add to the mix two poems associated with the deaths of kings in the late tenth century: the anonymous *Eiríksmál* "Words of Eiríkr," and *Hákonarmál* "Words of Hákon," assigned to the poet Eyvindr Finnsson. Eiríkr blóðøx "bloodaxe" and Hákon inn góði "the good" were Norwegian kings in the second half of the ninth century, and these poems deal with their accession to Valhǫll (for the texts see "Resources" later in this book). Thus a mythology of Óðinn as god of kings, warriors, and death figures in them. Because the poets chose to use the less strict meter of eddic poems, the built-in opposition to change that typified the more ornate *dróttkvætt* poems is lacking, and we can hardly be sure that the poets' original words have come down to us. Conceptually, however, it seems likely that the poems do reflect the mythology of Óðinn, even if the notion of "sacred text" is difficult to apply to a poem intended to praise a king, in this case by explaining his death as the will of Óðinn gathering troops for Ragnarøk.

As has been noted several times, the eddic poems as we have them are unlikely to be verbatim examples of sacred narrative, since they had presumably been undergoing change in oral transmission for over two centuries after the conversion to Christianity before they were written down. And as also has been noted, they reflect a deep history that was probably noted as early as by Tacitus in the end of the first century CE. A few scholars have advanced the idea that some of the eddic poems may have been composed by Christian poets after the conversion to Christianity, but it is difficult to imagine circumstances under which such composition could have taken place, specifically what exactly the impetus and audience might have been to give rise to the creation of new plots. *Þrymskviða* was for a while the poster child for late composition, given Þórr's cross-dressing, but the plot of the theft of the thunder weapon is widespread and ancient, and the hyper-masculinity that creates the tension around Þórr's disguise runs throughout the mythology. Another candidate for late composition was *Lokasenna*, since the gods are ridiculed, but it is possible to "verify" many of Loki's claims, and the form of the verbal duel was a staple of eddic poetry. Probably the most fruitful way to think about eddic poetry and the issue of sacred narrative, then, is to accept that the form is recent but that the content is old.

On that basis it will be fruitful to review what some of the subjects of sacred narrative in this form will have been—I say, "some of," because we have very clear indications of now lost eddic poems, and even if we did not, we would postulate their existence. On this basis, we can contemplate the range of subjects that were treated in the sacred narratives of the Vikings.

First we must note the testimony of *Hymiskviða* to the existence of eddic poetry about Þórr's fishing expedition, which the *dróttkvætt* poetry and visual evidence shows to have been prominent during the Viking Age. The theft and reacquisition of the thunder-weapon (*Þrymskviða*) has just been mentioned. *Alvíssmál* suggests that Þórr could act in the slot of the one who triumphs in a verbal duel, and if that role seems strange for Þórr based on the rest of the material that has survived, the goal certainly does not: Þórr is protecting one of the females of the gods from sexual exploitation by the member of an out-group, as we have seen him do with Freyja on more than once occasion. Many commentators on the poem suggest that the dwarf suitor Alvíss might once have been a giant, and plausible as that is, we should evaluate the claim not only on the basis of conceptions of the roles of giants and dwarfs in the extant materials but also on the fact that considerable variation is to be expected.

We should also note the lack of a surviving eddic poem about Þórr's journey to Geirrøðr, the subject of Eilífr's *Þórsdrápa*. Given that both Snorri and Saxo have versions of the story, and that versions of Snorri's *Edda* quote two eddic stanzas, we can hardly deny that this myth will have circulated in eddic verse form;[1] here is something close to proof that we have lost substantial amounts of eddic verse. The two verses that remain are embedded in Snorri's version of the story in manuscripts of *Skáldskaparmál*. Both report dialogue spoken by Þórr. The first occurs, Snorri says, when Þórr is halfway through the river and it is rising perilously high.

> "Rise not thou now, Vimur, since I desire to wade thee into the giants' courts. Know thou that if thou risest then will rise the Asstrength in me up as high as heaven."[2] [Faulkes 1987: 82]

The line "At its outlet must a river be stemmed," spoken by Þórr when he casts a rock at the giantess straddling the river and swelling it, may also have been a line from the same lost poem.

But we have another whole stanza from the Uppsala manuscript of Snorri's *Edda*, placed in the narrative just after Þórr has pressed down the chair on which he is sitting as the daughters of Geirrøðr attempt to lift it and smash him against the roof:

---

[1] As was noted earlier, this myth was also encapsulated into two *dróttkvætt* stanzas describing a brawl, and it was "displaced" into the fantastic *Þorsteins þáttr bœjarmagns*. For a discussion of the implication of these variations on modes of mythic narrative, see Lindow 2014.

[2] The first component in the compound "As-strength" has the root of the word for gods, *Æsir*, and the compound thus refers to what we might term "divine strength."

Once I used
all my strength
in giants' courts,
when Gjálp and Gneip,[3]
daughters of Geirrøðr,
tried to lift me to the sky. [Heimir Pálsson and Faulkes 2012: 97]

We can surmise that in this lost eddic poem about Þórr's journey to Geirrøðr's courts, Þórr's threat to rise up with his divine strength, in the other extant stanza, was made good in the episode with Geirrøðr's daughters.

The only major myth of Þórr of which we know that has not left traces in preserved eddic poetry is therefore the duel with Hrungnir. Þjóðólfr's *Haustlǫng* was based on a painted or decorated shield, but what was the source of the images? It makes sense to postulate an eddic poem that left not one or two but no stanzas.

As we have seen, Þórr predominates in the pre-Christian *dróttkvætt* poetry that has been preserved. Eddic poetry has a far wider range of subjects, for which we may be grateful. Indeed, our notions of Óðinn come primarily from eddic poetry, and of course from Snorri. It is not difficult to imagine that the poets who kept the *dróttkvætt* form alive (and probably also the eddic form) after the conversion to Christianity paid special heed to Óðinn.

Strictly speaking, then, the concept of myth as sacred narrative is quite problematized in the case of Old Norse mythology. It appears that the closest we can come to confidence about the actual wording of sacred texts is for the most part limited to poems that are actually (or in some cases are likely to have been) descriptions of images on objects. When we know the context for the performance of such poetry, as in the case of *Húsdrápa* being performed at a wedding which

---

[3] It is a sign of the prevailing acceptance of variation that Heimir Pálsson, the most recent editor of this text, has let stand the name form *Gneip*. Previous generations of editors would have changed it to *Greip*, the main form in the other manuscripts.

was the first formal event in a new hall with decorations, we cannot directly associate the narrative with ritual directed to the deity in question. A particularly important issue in this context is the lack of any evidence for the worship of Loki, who as we just saw has a larger presence in the extant *dróttkvætt* poetry than does Óðinn.

We do have the three fragments addressed to Þórr, those of Bragi, Vetrliði Sumarliðason, and Þorbjǫrn dísarskáld, introduced in chapter 2. The chronological spread, from the first skald to the last pre-Christian skalds, and the geographic spread, with both Norway and Iceland represented, suggests perhaps that there was once quite a lot of this kind of verse, and indeed it is difficult to imagine that there were no rituals at all that did not address the gods directly. These are certainly sacred texts, but they are not narrative, although they definitely must allude to narratives.

Chapter 3 showed how medieval intellectual models were applied to Old Norse mythology. Had demonization been the only model applied, our knowledge of the mythology would be scant, because the gods were simply names that were plugged into well-worn Christian narratives. Euhemerization, however, was quite the opposite: here the old myths were plugged into a theory of history. Euhemerism stripped the myths of their sacral nature and therefore allowed them to survive down to our day by being recorded on parchment. We see euhemerism as far back as the early twelfth-century Icelandic priest and historian Ari Þorgilsson, who could trace his genealogy not just to pagan ancestors in Iceland but ultimately to Freyr. It may well be possible that such euhemerist (or perhaps just historical?) thinking preceded the arrival of medieval learning in the North. That would be the case if what mattered was not so much descent from the gods as descent from kings. In Ari's case, the kings were Yngvi of Troy and Njǫrðr of the Svíar. Even if the conversion to Christianity established that Yngvi-Freyr and Njǫrðr (and Óðinn) were not and could never have been divine, their status as kings and ancestors could remain. If foolish and ignorant people had chosen to worship these kings as gods, that did not diminish such status.

The kings of more recent times (those whom we would call historical) were celebrated in poetry, namely that special kind of poetry that we call *dróttkvætt*. As I have mentioned more than once, that poetry would have been unintelligible without knowledge of the myths and heroic legends that underlie the kennings that are the heart, the very essence, of that poetry. Poets thus must have had to separate the myths from any sacral context, and some form of euhemerism would clearly have been useful for that purpose: like Sigurðr the dragon-slayer or Gunnarr in the snake pit, Óðinn and the Æsir were not dangerous if they were just men who had lived long ago and done special things. Perhaps there were other strategies, too: in the twenty-first century it is not difficult to imagine poets saying the old myths were "just stories," the "fake news" of the time (although the Church may have insisted on higher standards for dismissing unpleasant or awkward stories than are applied today). But whatever the strategy, the point was to desacralize the myths so that they were not sacred narratives and thus could continue to confer meaning on verse old and new. Perhaps here we have an explanation for the prominence of ekphrasis in what has survived in pre-Christian *dróttkvætt* poetry: as a description of an image on an object, an ekphrasis is one remove from a sacred narrative. One might say that the poet verbalizes an image, not a myth.

According to the theory I am advancing here, then, eddic poems survived—had to survive—because they were the old traditional depositories of myth and heroic legend. The mythological eddic poems were reborn as non-sacred narratives that underlay an important part of the kenning system. That *dróttkvætt* poetry celebrated and thus was the property of kings and important families would certainly have eased in the de-sacralization of the apparatus surrounding it, and I would argue that eddic poetry survived because it comprised an important part of that apparatus. Before Snorri systematized the kenning system and broke down the myths into discrete elements, skalds probably learned how to understand and create kennings not only from *dróttkvætt* poetry but also from eddic poetry.

Christianity brought the need to strip the myths of their sacred component, but it also actually brought the concept of strict separation of the sacred and the non-sacred. To put it another way, in pre-Christian Scandinavian society, as in other "primary" religions— those that do not have a canon and in which, therefore, dogma and belief are far less important that the proper conduct of rituals[4]—the distinction between what belonged to religion and what did not was scarcely perceptible. By some measures, virtually everything belonged to religion. Some aspects of life may have connected more closely than others to the numinous, but there simply was no sharp divide, as there is in secondary religions—those with a canon— between the religious and the non-religions. This understanding of the relationship between religion and human life is very much a product of the twenty-first century; the great twentieth-century religious thinkers, such as Nathan Söderblom, Rudolf Otto, Émile Durkheim, Max Scheler, and finally Mircea Eliade, all operated with a strong binary—as Eliade codified it, the sacred and the profane. But as we now understand Viking Age religion, there was no such binary. All aspects of life connected with the gods to a greater or lesser extent.

Thus, although Christianity exempted Old Norse mythology from the realm of the sacred in its dichotomous system and did so as an important tenet of the Christianization of the North, it did not deprive it of its importance. The connection to the history and traditions of those in power was simply too great for that to happen. So dominant was *dróttkvætt* poetry among the ruling elite that, for example, the miracles following the death of St Óláfr Haraldsson were detailed in *dróttkvætt* by a skald just a few years after his death, and when Niðarós was declared an archbishopric for Norway and the Atlantic islands in 1152–1153, the Icelandic skald Einarr Skúlason composed and recited before the archbishop and

---

[4] The distinction was put forward by Jan Assmann; see, for example, Assmann 2006.

Norway's joint kings an elaborate *dróttkvætt* poem about the saint. It was not until the thirteenth century that Christian poets began to innovate and suggest that they could compose *dróttkvætt* poetry without the kennings of the *Edda*—that is, the kennings that Snorri had codified.

During the Icelandic Middle Ages, Old Norse mythology may not have been literally sacred, but it may have been metaphorically so, through an ideological link to matters of the highest importance. The ideological use of the mythology, which as we saw in chapter 4 went back to pre-Christian times, can be seen as parallel to or akin to its sacred use before the conversion to Christianity. In the Middle Ages it served, indirectly perhaps, the ruling elite of both state and church. From the early modern period through national romanticism, it served national and patriotic interests by offering, in euhemerized form, deep national history. The continued use of the mythology in all sorts of media shows that even if the Old Norse myths are no longer sacred narratives, they remain good to think with.

SUGGESTIONS FOR FURTHER READINGS

Comprehensive works offering treatment of the social, historical, and literary contexts in which the myths circulated, both pre-Christian and Christian, include Stefan Brink, ed., in collaboration with Neil Price, *The Viking World* (2008); Knut Helle, ed., *The Cambridge History of Scandinavia*, vol. 1: *Prehistory to 1520* (2003); Philipp Pulsiano and Kirsten Wolf, eds., *Medieval Scandinavia: An Encyclopedia* (1993); Kirsten Hastrup, *Culture and History in Medieval Iceland* (1985); Margaret Clunies Ross, ed., *Old Icelandic Literature and Society* (2000); and Rory McTurk, ed., *A Companion to Old Norse Literature and Culture* (2005).

Several good handbooks of the mythology exist using a dictionary format. They differ in aim and coverage.

John Lindow, *Norse Mythology: A Guide to the Gods, Heroes, Rituals, and Beliefs* (Oxford, 2001), contains a chapter on "Time," in which a few pages treat the subject of chapter 1 in this work, but at far shorter length. Ch. 4 "Print and Non-Print Resources" overlaps with the present section but does not, of course, reflect the most recent scholarship. The bulk of *Norse Mythology* consists of a dictionary-like listing of entries on gods and important mythological topics. It differs from other handbooks in emphasizing first what the texts themselves say, before moving on to a synopsis of the scholarship.

Rudolf Simek, *Dictionary of Northern Mythology* (1993), is a translation of *Lexikon der germanischen Mythologie* (1984); thus the emphasis is Germanic, not Norse. The difference is not big in this case, but it means that the point of view is slightly different and, more important, that it casts a wider net. Thus entries tend to be shorter than those in Lindow. A strength of this dictionary, besides the scope and the excellent scholarship, is the inclusion of representations of relevant motifs in plastic art.

Andy Orchard, *Dictionary of Norse Myth and Legend* (1997), treats not only mythological topics but also heroic legend; the entries are therefore generally significantly shorter than those in Lindow's handbook. The scholarship is sound.

A fairly comprehensive annotated bibliography treating works up to the early 1980s is John Lindow, *Bibliography of Scandinavian Mythology* (1988).

A standard handbook of Old Norse mythology, presented in the context of religion, remains the comprehensive treatment of Germanic religion by Jan de Vries, *Altgermanische Religionsgeschichte* (1956–1957). Although some of its interpretive paradigms may no longer hold, its systematic treatment and thorough treatment make it invaluable. Also excellent and highly recommended even for those who can read the German of de Vries is Gabriel Turville-Petre, *Myth and Religion of the North* (1964). Thomas A. DuBois, *Nordic Religions in the Viking Age* (1999), offers a stimulating presentation of aspects of the religious traditions that met during the Viking Age: the Old Norse religion that is the subject of this book, the religion of the Sámi people, and the new religion, Christianity. A recent wide-ranging recent presentation is Carolyne Larrington, *The Norse Myths: A Guide to the Gods and Heroes* (2017).

Both de Vries and Turville-Petre were rather influenced by the theories of Geroges Dumézil, and they have faded somewhat in recent times. Nevertheless, the Indo-European component remains important, and it can be grasped in M. L. West, *Indo-European Poetry and Myth* (2007). Rather than put the material into a large structural framework, as Dumézil did, West organizes his presentation into a series of shorter presentations that clearly present the data.

A new comprehensive multi-author treatment of Old Scandinavian religion, including both mythology and ritual, and based more than previous surveys on a far wider variety of sources—especially archaeology—is Jens Peter Schjødt, John Lindow, and Anders Andrén, eds., *The Pre-Christian Religions of the North: History and Structures* (2020). Vol. 3 of this four-volume work comprises a survey of various mythological subjects: cosmogony, cosmology, eschatology, all various gods about whom we have any significant knowledge, and other mythological beings.

The mythology receives systematic analysis in Margaret Clunies Ross, *Prolonged Echoes*, vol. 1: *The Myths* (1994), and, from a rather different perspective, in Christopher Abram, *Myths of the Pagan North* (2011). I highly recommend both for anyone looking to delve deeper into Old Norse mythology. Clunies Ross, *Prolonged Echoes*, vol. 2: *The Reception of Norse Myths in Medieval Iceland* (1998), explores continued use of mythic patterns in medieval Iceland during the period when the myths were recorded.

An excellent recent handbook treating all aspects of eddic poetry is Carolyne Larrington, Judy Quinn, and Brittany Schorn, eds., *A Handbook to Eddic Poetry* (2016). While I prefer and have cited Larrington's revised translation (2014), which I find to be the most accurate, with the best introduction, and the added virtue of including separately both versions of *Vǫluspá*, other good translations exist: Ursula Dronke, *The Poetic Edda*, vols. 2–3, *Mythological Poems* (1997 and 2011), and Andy Orchard, *The Elder Edda* (2011). Jeramy Dodds, *The Poetic Edda* (2011), sacrifices direct accuracy for a more poetic idiom, and Jackson Crawford, *The Poetic Edda* (2015), aims for a more contemporary idiom (this book also includes a "Cowboy Hávamál"). Readers who wish to gain a deeper understanding of *dróttkvætt* poetry will profit from the insightful presentation of Roberta Frank, *Old Norse Court Poetry* (1978). Nothing comparable to the *Handbook to Eddic Poetry* exists for Snorri's *Edda*, although the commentary to *Gylfaginning* by Gottfried Lorenz (1984) can be helpful for those who read German, even though the references are no longer up to date. Kevin J. Wanner, *Snorri Sturluson and the Edda* (2008), suggests a context for understanding Snorri Sturluson's drive to preserve and systematize the older poetry.

Numerous sites on the web treat the subject of Old Norse mythology. They vary in quality, but because they do not go through the kind of peer review and rigorous editing that academic print works do, they lack the rigor of such works.

Comprehensive treatment of ritual in the Old Norse sources and in Old Scandinavian society is to be found in Jens Peter Schjødt, *Initiation between Two Worlds* (2008). In *Tracing Old Norse Cosmology* (2014), Anders Andrén uses archaeological materials to explore the development of certain concepts of mythic cosmology over time.

Two books that treat both Old Norse mythology and its reception are Heather O'Donoghue, *From Asgard to Valhalla* (2007), and Martin Arnold, *Thor: Myth to Marvel* (2011). Both are sound on Old Norse mythology and engaging on the reception: O'Donoghue offers particularly perceptive readings of various literary works and Arnold of what I here call the ideological use of materials. Focused exclusively on reception and equally rewarding are the chapters on Old Norse mythology in Jón Karl Helgason, *Echoes of Valhalla* (2017). For the reception of Old Norse mythology in English poetry, see the thorough treatment by Heather O'Donoghue, *English Poetry and Old Norse Myth: A History* (2014). During the 1990s, an international project was focused on the reception of Old Norse mythology; for a report see Margaret Clunies Ross and Lars Lönnroth, "The Norse Muse" (1999). A new multi-author presentation of the history of research and reception of pre-Christian religion, and very relevant to chapters 3 and 4, is the two-volume set edited by Margaret Clunies Ross: *The Pre-Christian Religions of the North: Research and Reception*. Vol. 1 covers the period *From the Middle Ages to c. 1830* (Clunies Ross 2018a); vol. 2 covers the period *From c. 1830 to the Present* (Clunies Ross 2018b).

Highly relevant to ch. 4, and worth reading in any case for its suggestive definition of "myth as ideology in narrative form," is Bruce Lincoln, *Theorizing Myth* (1999). The core of the book is a discussion of the role of ideology in the formation of scholarship about mythology, not least in the Germanic area (Lincoln 1999: 47–140). Also relevant is the ecocritical analysis of Christopher Abrams, *Evergreen Ash: Ecology and Catastrophe in Old Norse Myth and Literature* (2019).

The study of Old Norse mythology has experienced something of a revival in the last decades, and one sign of this revival has been a series of conferences, seminars, and symposia on the subject. The papers (all of them in English) from some of these have been published in separate volumes. These include Margaret Clunies Ross, ed., *Old Norse Myths, Literature and* Society (2003), Anders Andrén, Kristina Jennbert, and Catharine Raudvere, eds. *Old Norse Religion in Long-Term Perspectives* (2006); Catharina Raudvere and Jens Peter Schjødt, eds., *More than Mythology* (2012); Timothy R. Tangherlini, ed., *Nordic Mythologies: Interpretations, Intersections, and Institutions* (2014); Stefan Brink and Lisa Collinson, eds., *Theorizing Old Norse Myth* (2017); Pernille Hermann, Stephen A. Mitchell, and Jens Peter Schjødt, eds., *Old Norse Mythology: Comparative Perspectives* (2017); and Klas Wikström af Edholm et al., eds. *Myth, Materiality, and Lived Religion: In Merovingian and Viking Scandinavia* (2019). To these may be added a few other collections of essays, many of which have to do with Old Norse mythology: Judy Quinn, Kate Heslop, and Tarrin Wills, eds., *Learning and Understanding in the Old Norse World* (2007); Merrill Kaplan and Timothy R. Tangherlini, eds., *News from Other Worlds* (2012); and Irene García Losquiño, Olof Sundqvist, and Declan Taggart, eds., *Making the Profane Sacred in the Viking Age* (2020). Numerous relevant analyses by John McKinnell are collected in his *Essays on Eddic Poetry* (2014).

Some relevant specialist books in English include John Lindow, *Murder and Vengeance among the Gods: Baldr in Scandinavian Mythology* (1997); Richard Perkins, *Thor the Wind-Raiser and the Eyrarland Image* (2001); Olof Sundqvist, *Freyr's Offspring: Rulers and Religion in Ancient Svea Society (2002)*; John McKinnell, *Meeting the Other in Norse Myth and Legend* (2005); Clive Tolley, *Shamanism in Norse Myth and* Magic (2009); Karen Bek-Pedersen, *The Norns in Old Norse Mythology* (2011); Declan Taggart, *How Thor Lost His Thunder* (2018); and Neil Price, *The Viking Way: Magic and Mind in Late Iron Age Scandinavia* (2019).

RESOURCES

This section is intended to enable the reader to examine at first hand texts and artifacts and images that exemplify important aspects of Old Norse mythology and the problems of interpretation they present.

Texts

Entry into Valhǫll

In 954, Eiríkr blóðøx "bloodax," one of the sons of Haraldr hárfagri "fairhair" and ruler of York, died at the battle of Stainmore. Shortly thereafter his wife Gunnhildr commissioned the poem Eiríksmál, now anonymous, describing Eiríkr's arrival in Valhǫll and, in st. 7, indicating that his defeat was a deliberate choice by Óðinn to add Eiríkr to his forces before Ragnarøk should occur. It is likely that the poem (which may or may not be complete in its current form) retains pre-Christian conceptions about Valhǫll and its inhabitants. Other than Óðinn and Eiríkr, the three named characters in Valhǫll are Bragi, Sigmundr, and Sinfjǫtli. Bragi is presumably the human poet Bragi Boddason, and Sigmundr and Sinfjǫtli are human heroes. Thus the poem would have reinforced conceptions of the afterlife for warriors and poets.

*Eiríkr had been driven out of Norway by his half-brother Hákon,
called both Aðalsteinsfóstri "foster-son of Aðalstan" (king of England,
where Hákon became Christian) and inn góði "the good." Hákon
ruled over much of Norway until his death in the battle of Fitjar (on
the island Stord near the mouth of the Hardanger fjord in south-
west Norway) c. 961. According to Snorri's saga about Hákon in
Heimskringla (Hákonar saga góða), as he lay near death Hákon
lamented the fact that he would be unable to die among Christians
but bade the heathens around him to bury him as they chose. Snorri
continues as follows:*

> *There they raised a great mound and in it buried the king in full armor
> and in his finest array, but with no other valuables. Words were spoken
> over his grave according to the custom of heathen men, and they put
> him on the way to Valhalla. Eyvind Skáldaspillir composed a poem
> about the fall of King Hákon and how he was welcomed [in Valhalla].
> It is called Hákonarmál. [Hollander 1964: 124–25]*

*Eyvindr Finnsson was an active poet in the courts of several rulers, in-
cluding Hákon inn góði. His panegyric to the recently deceased ruler
emphasizes the king's prowess in battle but ends up covering some of the
same ground as the shorter anonymous Eiríksmál. It is believed that this
overlap, as well as a similar case, and the lines that open st. 21 being
known from elsewhere, gave Eyvindr his cognomen: "skáldaspillir," literally "destroyer of poets" but perhaps better "despoiler of poets," that is,
"plagiarist." That may well be, but his conception of Valhǫll seems more
complex and perhaps darker than that of Eiríksmál. The army is dispir-
ited going there, and Hákon worries about Óðinn's disposition (perhaps
because Hákon is Christian?). In the end he is welcome, and Eyvindr tells
the audience that Hákon had maintained the cult (st. 18).*

*Taken together, these poems suggest that conceptions of Óðinn,
Valhǫll and the einherjar, Ragnarøk, and the mythologizing of recently
deceased kings were current during the second half of the tenth century. In that light, these poems may be thought of as sacred texts within*

the mythological system that was later to be recorded as Old Norse mythology.

Eiríksmál [Fulk 2012a]

1 *Óðinn*: "What kind of dream is this, that I thought that a little before daybreak I was preparing Valhǫll for a slain army? I awakened the *einherjar*, I asked them to get up to strew the benches, to rinse the drinking cups, [I asked] valkyries to bring wine, as if a leader should come."

2 "I expect certain glorious men from the world [of the living], so my heart is glad."

3 *Bragi*: "What is making a din there, as if a thousand were in motion, or an exceedingly great throng? All the bench-planks creak, as if Baldr were coming back into Óðinn's residence."

4 *Óðinn*: "The wise Bragi must not talk nonsense, though you know well why: the clangout is made for Eiríkr, who must be coming in here, a prince into Óðinn's residence."

5 *Óðinn:* "Sigmundr and Sinfjǫtli, rise quickly and go to meet the prince. Invite [him] in, if it is Eiríkr; it is he I am expecting now."

6 *Sigmundr*: "Why do you expect Eiríkr rather than other kings?" *Óðinn:* "Because he has reddened his blade in many a land and borne a bloody sword."

7 *Sigmundr*: "Why did you deprive him of victory then, when he seemed to you to be valiant?" *Óðinn:* "Because it cannot be known for certain when the grey wolf will attack the home of the gods."

8 *Sigmundr*: "Good fortune to you now, Eiríkr; you will be welcome here, and go, wise, into the hall. One thing I want to ask you: what princes accompany you from the edge-thunder [BATTLE]?"

9 *Eiríkr*: "There are five kings; I shall identify for you the names of all; I am myself the sixth."

Eyvindr skáldaspillir Finnsson, Hákonarmál *[Fulk 2012b]*

1 The god of the Gautar [=Óðinn] sent Gǫndul and Skǫgul to choose among kings, which of the kin of Yngvi should go with Óðinn and live in Valhǫll.

2 They [the valkyries] found Bjǫrn's brother [=Hákon] putting on a mail-shirt, that admirable king, stationed under his battle-standard. Enmity-yard-arms [SPEARS] drooped, and the banner shook; the battle was then begun.

3 The sole slayer of jarls [=Hákon] called on the Háleygir just as on the Hólmrygir; he went into battle. The munificent terrifier of island-Danes [=Hákon] had the good support of the Norwegians; he stood under a helmet of metal.

4 The leader of the retinue [Hákon] threw off his war-garments [ARMOUR], cast his mail-shirt to the ground, before beginning the battle. The cheerful ruler joked with his men; he had to protect the land; he stood under a golden helmet.

5 Then the sword in the sovereign's hand bit the garments of Váfuðr <=Óðinn>[ARMOUR], as if it were cutting through water. Points clanged, shields burst, swords clattered in men's skulls.

6 Shields [and] Norwegians' skulls were trampled under the hard feet of hilts [SWORDS] of the Týr <god> of rings [MAN]. Battle arose on the island; kings reddened gleaming shield-fortresses in the blood of men.

7 Wound-fires [SWORDS] burned in bloody wounds; swords swung down on men's lives. The wound-sea [BLOOD] roared on the headland of swords [SHIELD]; the flood of barbs [BLOOD] fell on the shore of Stord.

8 Red colours mingled beneath the sky of the shield-rim [SHIELD]; the storms of Skǫgul <valkyrie> [BATTLE] played against the clouds of shield-rings [SHIELDS]. Point-waves [BLOOD] roared in the storm of Óðinn [BATTLE]; many people sank down before the tide of the sword [BLOOD].

9 Then kings were sitting with swords drawn, with hacked shields and pierced mail-shirt. That army was not in good spirits and was on its way to Valhǫll.

10 Gǫndul said that [this], leaned on a spear-shaft: "The gods' force grows now, since the gods have invited Hákon home with a great army."

11 The leader heard what the renowned valkyrie said from [on] horseback; they behaved prudently and remained, helmeted, and held shields in front of them.

12 "Why did you decide the battle thus, Spear-Skǫgul, though we were [I was] worthy of victory from the gods?" "We brought it about that you held the field and your enemies fled."

13 "We two shall ride," said the mighty Skǫgul, "through the green abodes of the gods, to say to Óðinn that now a supreme ruler will come to look on him in person."

14 "Hermóðr and Bragi," said Hroptatýr [Óðinn], "go to meet the monarch, because a king is coming here to the hall who is deemed a champion."

15 The ruler [Hákon] said that [this]—he had come from battle, stood all drenched in blood—: "Óðinn appears to us [me] to be very hostile; we [I] fear his intentions."

16 "You shall have quarter from all the *einherjar*; take ale among the Æsir. Adversary of jarls [RULER = Hákon], you have eight brothers in this place," said Bragi.

17 "We ourselves [I myself] wish to keep our [my] armour," said the good king; "one should take good care of one's helmet and mail-shirt; it is good to have recourse to ready gear."

18 It was revealed then how well that king had revered the sanctuaries, when all the guiding and ruling powers bade Hákon welcome.

19 On a good day will that monarch be born who gets for himself such a character. His time will always be spoken of as good.

20 The wolf Fenrir, unbound, will enter the abode of men before so good a royal person comes onto the vacant path.

21   Livestock are dying, kinsfolk are dying, land and realm be-
     come deserted, since Hákon went with the heathen gods;
     many a nation is enslaved.

Lokasenna (Loki's Quarrel) [Larrington 2014: 80–92]

*Lokasenna is the eighth poem in the Poetic Edda, located between
Hymiskviða and Þrymskviða, both of which feature Þórr as the protagonist. The redactor presumably grouped Lokasenna with these poems because in the end it is only Þórr who can silence Loki, and he was able to
provide continuity by linking in the prose header ("About Ægir and the
Gods") the drinking feast to the cauldron that Þórr acquired in the previous poem, Hymiskviða (see chapter 2). Nevertheless, the story stands
alone and is one of many verbal duels in Old Norse poetry and saga literature. In this particular case the exchanges are short, with Loki usually
silencing each of his divine opponents by referring to some fact or event
that the deity would not wish to hear. In many cases these facts or events
are referred to elsewhere, and there is no reason to doubt the ones that are
unique to this poem. In other words, the gods had flaws, and people knew
about them, even if today we do not understand all of Loki's insults.*

*The concept of flawed gods, who behaved dishonorably or were
humiliated in some way, led some early readers of the poem to argue that
it could not have reflected some earlier sacred text, but rather that it must
have been composed in Christian times to malign the old gods. Scholars
are more cautious today, and there is no reason to deny out of hand the
possibility of a myth in which the enigmatic trickster figure Loki should
engage in an embarrassing verbal duel with the other gods. The message in the end is positive: Þórr restores order, and vengeance is taken on
Loki ("About Loki"). A version of this vengeance is also found in Snorri's
Gylfaginning, where it is enacted because of Loki's role in that version
of the death of Baldr. Here we should recall the legal provisions against
"fully chargeable offenses" discussed in chapter 1, a rubric under which
some of Loki's verbal statements might be grouped. Sacred text or not*

in its current form, Lokasenna is good to think with. It provides a con-
cise summary of a mythology that is fraught with moral ambiguity and
provides some fascinating information that is found in no other sources.

A note on the text: like many translators, Larrington sets in Italic the
prose sections of the text (the header, a few lines between stanzas, and the
ending about the vengeance taken on Loki). This practice indicates what
is verse and what is not and implies that prose sections do not belong to
the poem (for example, may have been added by the redactor of the manuscript). While that is possible, I prefer to show the text as we have it and
have therefore set the entirety in Roman.

The speaker attributions are abbreviated marginal notations, so those
I have left in Italic.

About Ægir and the Gods

Ægir, who is also called Gymir, had brewed ale for the Æsir, when he
got the great cauldron which has just been told about. To this feast
came Odin and Frigg, his wife. Thor did not come, because he was
away in the east. Sif was there, Thor's wife, Bragi, and Idunn, his wife.
Tyr was there; he was one-handed, for Fenrir the wolf tore his hand
off when he was bound. There was Niord and his wife, Skadi, Freyr
and Freyia, Vidar, son of Odin; Loki was there and the servants of
Freyr, Byggvir and Beyla. Many of the Æsir and elves were there.
Ægir had two servants, Fimafeng and Eldir. Shining gold was used
instead of firelight; ale went round by itself; that was a great place
of peace. People praised the excellence of Ægir's servers. Loki could
not bear to hear that, and he killed Fimafeng. Then the Æsir shook
their shields and shrieked at Loki and chased him out to the woods,
and they set to drinking.

Loki came back and met Eldir outside; Loki greeted him:

> 1   "Tell me, Eldir, before you step
>   a single foot forward,
>   what the sons of the victory-gods here inside
>   talk about over their ale."

Eldir said:

2   "They discuss their weapons and their readiness for war,
     the sons of the victory-gods;
     among the Æsir and elves who are within,
     no one has a friendly word for you."

Loki said:

3   "In I shall go, into Ægir's halls
     to have a look at that feast;
     quarrelling and strife I'll bring to the Æsir's sons
     and thus mix their mead with malice."

Eldir said:

4   "You know, if in you go, into Ægir's halls
     to have a look at that feast,
     if accusation and scandal you pour over the loyal gods,
     they'll wipe it off on you."

Loki said:

5   "You know, Eldir, that if you and I should
     contend with wounding words,
     I'll be rich in my replies
     when you say too much."

Afterwards Loki went into the hall. And when those inside saw who
had come in, they all fell silent.
Loki said:

6   "Thirsty I come to this hall,
     Loki, come a long way,

to ask the Æsir that they should give me
one drink of magnificent mead."

7 "Why are you so silent, you pride-swollen gods,
that you are unable to speak?
Assign me a place to sit at the feast,
or tell me to go away!"

Bragi said:

8 "A place to sit at the feast
the Æsir will never assign you,
for the Æsir know for whom they should
provide their potent feast."

Loki said:

9 "Do you remember, Odin, when in bygone days
we blended our blood together?
You said you'd never imbibe beer
unless it were brought to both of us."

Odin said:

10 "Get up then, Vidar, and let the wolf's father
sit down at the feast,
lest Loki speak words of blame
to us in Ægir's hall."

Then Vidar stood up and poured a drink for Loki, and before he
drank, he toasted the Æsir.

11 "Hail to the Æsir, hail to the Asynior
and all the most sacred gods!
—except for that one god who sits further in,
Bragi, on the benches."

Bragi said:

12   "A horse and a sword I'll give you from my possessions,
and Bragi will recompense you with a ring too,
so you don't repay the Æsir with hatred;
don't make the gods exasperated with you!"

Loki said:

13   "Both horses and arm-rings you'll always be short of, Bragi;
of the Æsir and the elves who are in here,
you're the wariest of war
and shyest of shooting."

Bragi said:

14   "I know if I were outside, just as now I am now inside
Ægir's hall,
your head I'd be holding in my hand;
I'd see that as reward for your lies."

Loki said:

15   "You're brave in your seat, but you won't be doing that,
Bragi the bench-ornament!
You go and fight, if you are so furious,
the truly bold man doesn't think twice!"

Idunn said:

16   "I beg you, Bragi, that kin ties will hold
between the children and those who are adopted,
so you shouldn't speak words of blame to Loki
in Ægir's hall."

Loki said:

17   "Be silent, Idunn, I declare that of all women
      you're the most man-mad,
      since you wound your arms, washed bright,
      around your brother's killer."

Idunn said:

18   "I'm not speaking words of blame to Loki
      in Ægir's hall;
      I am quitening Bragi, made talkative with beer;
      I don't want you two angry men to fight."

Gefion said:

19   "Why should you two Æsir in here
      fight with wounding words?
      isn't it known of Loki that he likes a joke
      and all the gods love him?"

Loki said:

20   "Be silent, Gefion, I'm going to mention this,
      how your spirit was seduced;
      this white boy gave you a jewel
      and you laid your thigh over him."

Odin said:

21   "Mad you are, Loki, and out of your wits,
      when you make Gefion angry with you,
      for I think she knows all the fate of the world,
      as clearly as I myself."

Loki said:

22   "Be silent, Odin, you could never apportion war-fortune
     among men;
         often you've given what you shouldn't have given,
         victory, to the faint-hearted."

Odin said:

23   "You know, if I gave what I shouldn't have given,
         victory, to the faint-hearted,
         yet eight winters you were, beneath the earth,
         a milchcow and a woman,
         and there you bore children,
         and that I thought the hallmark of a pervert."

Loki said:

24   "But you, they say, practiced *seid* on Samsey,
         and you beat on the drum as seeresses do,
         in the likeness of a wizard you journeyed over mankind,
         and that I thought that the hallmark of a pervert."

Frigg said:

25   "The fates you met should never be
         told in front of people,
         what you two Æsir underwent in past times;
         the living should keep their distance from ancient matters."

Loki said:

26   "Be silent, Frigg, you're Fiorgyn's daughter
         and you've always been man-mad:

Ve and Vili, Vidrir's wife,
you took them both in your embrace."

Frigg said:

27   "You know that if I had in here in Ægir's hall
a boy like my son Baldr,
you wouldn't get away from the Æsir's sons;
there'd be furious fighting against you."

Loki said:

28   "Frigg, you want me to say more about my wicked deeds;
for I brought it about that you will never again
see Baldr ride to the halls."

Freyia said:

29   "Mad are you, Loki, when you reckon up your
ugly, hateful deeds;
Frigg knows, I think, all fate,
though she herself does not speak out."

Loki said:

30   "Be silent, Freyia, I know all about you;
you aren't free of faults:
of the Æsir and the elves, who are in here,
each one has been your lover."

Freyia said:

31   "False is your tongue, I think that soon
it will chant out disaster for you;

the Æsir are furious with you, and the Asynior,
you'll go home discomfited."

Loki said:

32   "Be silent, Freyia, you're a witch
and much imbued with malice,
you were with your brother, all the cheerful gods
surprised you,
and then, Freyia, you farted."

Niord said:

33   "That's harmless, if a woman has a husband,
or a lover, or one of each;
what's surprising is that a pervert god comes here
and he has borne children!"

Loki said:

34   "Be silent, Niord, you were sent from here
eastwards as hostage to the gods;
the daughters of Hymir used you as a pisspot
and pissed in your mouth."

Niord said:

35   "That was my comfort, when I, from far away,
was sent as hostage to the gods,
that I fathered that son, whom no one hates
and is thought the protector of the Æsir."

Loki said:

36   "Stop now, Niord, keep some moderation!
I won't keep it secret any longer:
with your sister you got that son,
though that's no worse than might be expected."

Tyr said:

37　"Freyr is the best of all the bold riders
　　in the courts of the Æsir;
　　he makes no girl cry nor any man's wife,
　　and looses each man from captivity."

Loki said:

38　"Be silent, Tyr, you could never
　　deal straight between two people;
　　your right hand, I must point out,
　　is the one which Fenrir tore from you."

Tyr said:

39　"I've lost a hand, but you've lost the famous wolf;
　　evil brings pain to us both;
　　it's not pleasant for the wolf, who must in shackles
　　wait for the twilight of the gods."

Loki said:

40　"Be silent, Tyr, it happened that your wife
　　had a son by me;
　　not an ell of cloth nor a penny have you ever had
　　for this injury, you wretch."

Freyr said:

41　"A wolf I see lying before a river mouth,
　　until the Powers are torn asunder;
　　next you shall be bound—unless you fall silent—
　　smith of evil!"

Loki said:

> 42   "With gold you had Gymir's daughter bought
>   and so you gave away your sword;
>   but when Muspell's sons ride over Myrkwood,
>   you don't know then, wretch, how you'll fight."

Byggvir said:

> 43   "You know, if I had the lineage of Freyr,
>   and such a blessed dwelling,
>   smaller than marrow I'd have ground that hateful crow
>   and mangled all his limbs into pieces."

Loki said:

> 44   "What's that little creature I see wagging its tail
>   and snapping things up snappily?
>   At Freyr's ears you're always found
>   and twittering under the grindstones."

Byggvir said:

> 45   "Byggvir I'm called, and I'm said to be busy
>   by all the gods and men;
>   thus I'm proud here that Odin's sons are
>   all drinking ale together."

Loki said:

> 46   "Be silent, Byggvir, you could never
>   share out food among men;
>   and in the bench-straw they can never find you
>   when men are going to fight."

Heimdall said:

47   "Drunk you are, Loki, so that you're out of your wits,
      why don't you stop speaking?
      For too much drinking affects every man
      so he doesn't notice his talkativeness."

Loki said:

48   "Be silent, Heimdall, for you in bygone days
      a hateful life was decreed:
      a mucky back you must always have
      and watch as guard of the gods."

Skadi said:

49   "You're light-hearted, Loki; you won't for long
      play with your tail wagging free,
      for on a rock-edge, with your ice-cold son's guts,
      the gods shall bind you."

Loki said:

50   "You know, if on a rock-edge, with my ice-cold son's guts,
      the gods shall bind me,
      first and foremost I was at the killing
      when we seized Thiazi."

Skadi said:

51   "You know, if first and foremost you were at the killing
      when you seized Thiazi,
      from my sanctuaries and meadows cold counsel
      shall always come to you."

Loki said:

> 52   "Gentler in speech you were to Laufey's son
>   when you had me invited to your bed;
>   we must mention such things when we reckon up
>   our shameful deeds."

Then Sif went forward and poured out mead for Loki into a crystal goblet and said:

> 53   "Welcome, now, Loki, and take the crystal goblet
>   full of ancient mead,
>   you should rather admit, of the Æsir's children,
>   that Sif alone is blameless."

He took the horn and drank it down:

> 54   "You would be the only one, if you were so,
>   were cautious and reluctant with a man;
>   I know one—and I think I do know—
>   a lover beside Thor,
>   and that was the malevolent Loki."

Beyla said:

> 55   "All the mountain-range shakes; I think Thor must be
>   on his way from home;
>   he'll bring peace to the one who badmouths here
>   all the gods and men."

Loki said:

> 56   "Be silent, Beyla, you're Byggvir's wife
>   and much imbued with malice;
>   no worse disgrace came among the Æsir's children,
>   you dung-spattered dairy-maid."

Then Thor arrived and said:

57   "Be silent, perverse creature, my mighty hammer
        Miollnir shall deprive you of speech;
        your shoulder-rock I shall strike off your neck,
        and then your life will be gone."

Loki said:

58   "The son of Earth has now come in;
        why are you raging so, Thor?
        But you won't be daring when you must fight against
      the wolf,
        when he swallows Odin all up."

Thor said:

59   "Be silent, perverse creature, my mighty hammer
        Miollnir shall deprive you of speech;
        I shall throw you up on the roads to the east,
        afterwards no one will ever see you."

Loki said:

60   "Your eastern journeys you should never relate to people
        since in the thumb of a glove you crouched
        cowering, you hero!
        And then you didn't seem like Thor."

Thor said:

61   "Be silent, perverse creature, my mighty hammer
        Miollnir shall deprive you of speech;
        with my right hand I'll strike you, with Hrungnir's killer,
        so that every one of your bones will break."

Loki said:

62   "I intend to live for a good time yet,
     though you threaten me with a hammer;
     strong leather straps you thought Skrymir had,
     and you couldn't get at the food,
     and you starved, unharmed but hungry."

Thor said:

63   "Be silent, perverse creature, my mighty hammer
     Miollnir shall deprive you of speech;
     Hrungnir's killer will send you to hell,
     down below the corpse-gate."

Loki said:

64   "I spoke before the Æsir, I spoke before the Æsir's sons
     what my spirit urged me,
     but for you alone I shall go out,
     for I know that you do strike.

65   "Ale you brewed, Ægir, but you'll never again
     prepare a feast;
     all your possessions that are here inside—
     may flame play over them,
     and your back be burnt."

About Loki

And after that Loki hid himself in the waterfall of Franangr, in the shape of a salmon. There the Æsir caught him. He was bound with the guts of his son Nari. But his son Narfi turned into a wolf. Skadi took a poisonous snake and fastened it over Loki's face; poison dripped down from it. Sigyn, Loki's wife, sat there and held a basin under the poison. But when the basin was full, she carried the poison out; and meanwhile the poison fell on Loki. Then he writhed so violently at this that all the earth shook from it; those are now called earthquakes.

The Marriage(s) of Skaði

The following three texts give an indication of the variety of both tone and content of Old Norse mythological texts. In Gylfaginning, Snorri presents the verse exchange between Njǫrðr and Skaði almost as an aside to the catalogue of Æsir that the speaker Hár is enumerating before the Swedish king Gylfi/Gangleri (although Njǫrðr makes up a part of this catalogue, Skaði is missing from the corresponding category of goddesses that comes a few pages later). Based on the fact that Snorri includes in Gylfaginning only the last stanza of Skírnismál—the story of Freyr's wooing of Freyja—one might infer that there was a longer poem behind this brief exchange (the third stanza may not have been part of it, if it existed, since this stanza is a variant version of Grímnismál st. 11, spoken by Óðinn as he hangs over a fire and has visions of the cosmos). Saxo has moved the myth down to the human level, although the story takes place early in Danish (pre-)history. This passage from the first book of Saxo's Danish history tells of the great warrior king Hadingus and his wife Regnera. Although Hadingus's career was advanced along by the help of "an aged man with only one eye" (1.6.7), most scholars understand him as a displacement of the god Njǫrðr. Saxo uses different Latin meters for the two verses, but stripped to their essences, they clearly reflect (versions of) the Old Norse verses cited in Gylfaginning, and this fact could suggest that there never was a longer poem.

In the third stanza in the passage from Gylfaginning as well as in the variant that is Grímnismál st. 11, Skaði is referred to as "bright bride of the gods." The plural "gods" is clarified by the part of Ynglinga saga, ch. 8, referring to Skaði, and quoting two verses (st. 2–3) from the poet Eyvindr Finnsson skáldaspillir's Háleygjatal, a poem that enumerates the rulers of Hálogaland in Western Norway and ends, as Snorri notes following his citation of the verses, with Hákon jarl of Lade, who ruled Norway from c. 970–995. Thus this royal line (Hákon kept the old-fashioned term "jarl" rather than "king") traced its genealogy not just to Óðinn but also to Skaði. Although this notion has left few other traces and is rarely mentioned in most treatments of Old Norse mythology, it was clearly important in real human society and shows the variation that is characteristic of all oral mythologies.

Gylfaginning Snorri's Edda [Faulkes 1987: 23–24]

Niord has a wife called Skadi, daughter of the giant Thiassi. Skadi wants to have the home her father had had—this is in some mountains, a place called Thrymheim—but Niord wants to be near the sea. They agreed on this, that they should stay nine nights in Thrymheim and then alternate nines at Noatun. But when Niord came back to Noatun from the mountains he said this:

> "I hate mountains—not long was I there, just nine nights: wolves' howling I thought ugly compared with the swans' song."

Then Skadi said this:

> "I could not sleep on the sea's beds for the birds' screaming; he wakes me who comes from out at sea every morning, that gull."

Then Skadi went up into the mountain and lived in Thrymheim and generally travels on skis and carries a bow and shoots game. She is called ski-deity and ski-lady. As it says:

> It is called Thrymheim where Thiassi dwelt, that most mighty giant, but now Skadi, bright bride of gods, inhabits her father's old abode.

Saxo Grammaticus, Gesta Danorum 1.8.18–19 [Friis-Jensen and Fisher 2015: 69–71]

When his rival had been removed all was quiet and he discontinued his warfaring completely for many years; finally, pleading that he had spent ages cultivating the land when he should have been indulging in naval exploits (as though he believed belligerence pleasanter than peace) he began to criticize himself for his sloth in this strain:

> "Why do I linger in the shadows,
> enfolded by rugged hills,
> not following the waves as before?
> The challenging howl of the wolf-pack,
> cries of dangerous brutes,
> ever raised to heaven,
> the ungovernable ferocity of beasts,
> snatch all rest from my eyes.
> The desolate ridges are cheerless
> to hearts bent on sterner schemes.
> The unbending cliffs and harsh
> terrain oppress those whose hearts
> delight in the high seas.
> To sound out the straits with our oars,
> revel in plundered wealth,
> pursue for our coffers another's
> fortune and gloat over sea-loot
> would be a far finer business
> than haunting the winding forest
> tracks and barren ravines."

His wife loved the life of the countryside and therefore, sick of the morning choir of sea birds, revealed in these words how much contentment lay for her in roving the expanses of woodland:

> "The chant of the birds torments me lagging here on the shore,
> disturbing me with their jabber whenever I try to sleep.
> I hear the ceaseless roar and fury of the tide
> as it takes away the gentle repose from my slumbering eyes;
> there is no relaxation at night for the shrill chatter of the sea mew,
> dinning its stupid screech into my tender ears,

for it will not allow me to rest in my bed or be refreshed,
but ominously caws away in dismal modulations.
For me there's a safer and sweeter thing—to sport in the woods.
How could you crop a more meagre share of peace in light
or darkness than by tossing on the shifting deep?"

Snorri Sturluson, Ynglinga saga *ch. 8.*

(I follow Hollander's translation [1964: 12] for the prose but have replaced his translation of the verses with the far more accurate translation of Russell Poole [2012: 199–201].)

Njorth married a woman who was called Skathi. She would not have intercourse with him, and later married Óthin. They had many sons. One of them was called Sæming. About him, Eyvind Skáldaspillir composed these verses:

2   The shield-worshiped kinsman of the Æsir <gods> [= Óðinn] begat that tribute-bringer [JARL = Sæmingr] with the female from Járnviðr, when those renowned ones, the friend of warriors [= Óðinn] and Skaði [giantess], lived in the lands of the maiden of the bone of the sea [(*lit.* "maiden-lands of the bone of the sea") ROCK > GIANTESS > = Jǫtunheimar "Giant-lands"],

3   and the ski-goddess [= Skaði] bore many sons with Óðinn.

Earl Hákon the Mighty reckoned his pedigree from Sæming.

Images and Artifacts

The only new data relating to Old Norse mythology that turns up comes from archaeological research (which in turn is frequently the result of chance, as when, for example, a dig is undertaken before a construction project is begun). It is safe to say that most interpretation of images and artifacts as relating to Old Norse mythology departs from the textual materials; the exception would be an interpretation based largely on comparative evidence. There is always uncertainty of interpretation: a horse with eight legs is probably Sleipnir, but how are we to know that an artist did not add extra legs to convey a sense of speed? A man with what looks like a serpent on the end of his line is presumably Þórr, but we can never prove that it is not just a man hooking an eel for supper. As in many aspects of our cultural and intellectual life, there have been trends in this matter, with skepticism sometimes prevailing and at other times a willingness to accept links between text and artifact or image. We are currently in the latter trend, with the happy result that a large amount of data is being added to the study of Old Norse mythology. Even if (when?) a skeptical trend returns, the data in question will still be there for study.

In what follows I will present a few of the more interesting artifacts and images, adding to the discussion in the above chapters.

Gold Bracteates

Gold bracteates are small round disks of pressed gold, produced for the most part in Scandinavia during the fifth century CE. Although they are based on Roman coins, they are pierced or equipped with loops and were thus presumably worn as pendants. Some contain runic inscriptions, and the iconography developed into highly stylized forms. Interpretations of some of these decorative forms as based on older forms of Old Norse mythology go back to the nineteenth century and characterized the scholarship by and inspired by Karl Hauck, the dominant scholar in this field in the second half of the twentieth century.[1] More recently, doubts have arisen (Wicker

---

[1] Hauck's rate of publication was nothing short of extraordinary. Those seeking a summary notion of his thinking about the bracteates and who are undaunted by complicated German are advised to begin with Hauck 1992. The materials themselves are most easily accessed in Pesch 2007.

and Williams 2012), but because the bracteates are little known outside the academic world, it is important to present some of them and the (controversial) interpretations here.

Hauck was, first, convinced that the healing charm known as the *Second Merseburg charm* was reflected on the bracteates. It goes as follows:

> Phol and Wodan went to the forest.
> Then Balder's horse sprained its foot.
> Then Sinthgunt sang charms, and Sunna her sister;
> then Friia sang charms, and Volla her sister;
> then Wodan sang charms, as he well could:
> be it bone-sprain, be it blood-sprain, be it limb-sprain:
> bone to bone, blood to blood, limb to limb,
> so be they glued together. [Lindow 2001: 227]

The language of the charm is Old High German, and the manuscript containing it is from c. 900 CE, so the charm was presumably in circulation at that time; how old it may be is impossible to determine. It contains the German analogues of Frigg (Friia), Óðinn (Wodan), and Baldr (Balder) and attests a myth that is not known in Old Norse mythology, namely the gods, led by Óðinn, healing Baldr's horse. On this basis, Hauck and others see Óðinn and Baldr's horse on bracteates with an animal and human head, as in figure R.1. According to this interpretation, Óðinn is curing Baldr's horse by whispering into its ear.

Perhaps Baldr's death is also to be seen. The Faxe bracteate (figure R.2) contains an image of three men. Possibly Baldr stands in the center, between Loki and Hǫðr, as the fatal mistletoe is cast.

When one sees an image of a man with his hand in the mouth of a wolf, as on figure R.3, it is not difficult to imagine that we see Týr about to lose his hand to Fenrir. Whether that is what the artist

FIGURE R.1 Gold bracteate from Skåne, Sweden, dated to the fifth century, with a head (Óðinn?), a bird (one of his ravens?) and a horse (Baldr's lame horse?). From the Ashmoleon Museum's collection. Photo: HIP/Art Resource, NY.

intended, or how people who saw it in the fifth century and later understood it, is something we shall never know.

Gold Foil Figures

Gold foil figures are images pressed into tiny (no more than 2 cm) pieces of gold foil, dated from the sixth to the ninth centuries, often found around central places. Since they were deposited, among other places, in post holes, they may have had a ritual purpose. Gold foils from Denmark tend to have only one figure on them, those from Sweden and Norway two. When the two figures are embracing, as in figure R.4, they have been interpreted as representing Freyr and

FIGURE R.2 Gold bracteate from Faxe, dated to the fifth century (Nationalmuseet no. 8069). Photo: Kit Weiss, Nationalmuseet, København.

Gerðr. This is not the only plausible explanation, and we do not understand these relatively plentiful artifacts.

Ribe Skull Fragment

An unusual artifact dated to the eighth century is a fragment of a human skull unearthed in Ribe, Jylland, with a runic inscription (figure R.5).

Although the inscription defies definitive interpretation, the name Óðinn is contained in it, as well as words for "pain" and "dwarf," and scholars agree that it is likely to be a charm against head pain. Here, as in the *Second Merseburg Charm* mentioned above, we see Óðinn in a role associated with healing. Although healing is

FIGURE R.3 Rendering of the image on a bracteate from Trollhättan in Västergötland, dated to the fifth century (SHM 1164:109036). Drawing: Gunnar Creutz. Wikimedia Commons.

not central to the role of Óðinn in the mythology as we know it, in people's lives that must have been an important function of the god.

Gotland Picture Stones

While there are picture stones from all over Scandinavia, those from the island of Gotland occupy a special place in the study of Viking Age Scandinavia, including mythology. Gotlandic picture stones cover the period from c. 300–1100 CE, but it is some

FIGURE R.4 Gold foil figures from Helgö, Uppland, Statens Historiska Museum, Stockholm. Photo: Photo: HIP/Art Resource, NY.

of the later ones, from the ninth and tenth centuries, that are the most elaborately decorated. Several have numerous images framed in various panels, and a few of these seem to have fairly obvious mythological reference, some of which have been partially examined in chapters 1 and 2; Sleipnir seems particularly hard to miss, on the stones from both Ardre (figure 2.6) and Tjängvide (figure R.6)

Like Ardre, Tjängvide contains in the upper register an image of a rider (Óðinn? A dead hero?) on an eight-legged horse (Sleipnir?), with some kind of structure in the upper left (Valhǫll?). The rider on Tjängvide is being greeted by a woman with a drinking horn (a valkyrie? Freyja?). Beneath the structure, two figures appear to be battling (*einherjar*?).

Ardre and Tjängvide are unique in presenting the possible Sleipnir image, which is the clearest example of a motif that may

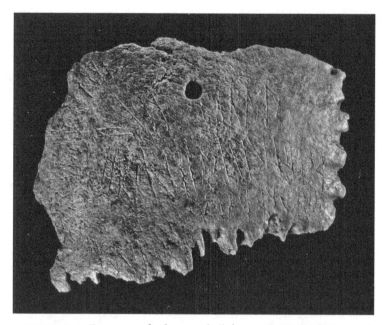

FIGURE R.5 Fragment of a human skull from Ribe, Jylland, Denmark, dated to the eighth century, with an incised runic inscription (DR EM85, 151B $, Samnordisk runtextdatabas). Photo: Lennart Larsen, Nationalmuseet, København.

perhaps be traced to the mythology. There are many other horses and riders on the Gotland picture stones, not to mention wagons and sleds and, most of all, ships, especially sailing ships on the stones from the eighth and ninth centuries. While these might conceivably have been linked to conceptions of the world of the dead, they might just as well be explained as objects of fascination in a maritime culture. Nevertheless, some images seem clearly to have to do with myth and ritual.

Figure R.7 shows the picture stone from Stora Hammars in Lärbro. In the middle of the third panel from the top, a sacrifice on an altar is taking place, and to the left an armed warrior hangs from a tree. The panel below may show the legend of an eternal battle

FIGURE R.6 The picture stone from Tjängvide, Gotland. The granite stone is 1.7 meters high and is conventionally dated to the eighth century. A memorial runic inscription is incised in the text band to the right of the ship. Wikimedia Commons. This file is licensed under the *Creative Commons* Attribution-Share Alike *4.0 International, 3.0 Unported, 2.5 Generic, 2.0 Generic,* and *1.0 Generic* license.

between two armies, supposedly caused by Freyja, and the bottom panel may show the death of the hero Sigurðr.

The Gotland picture stones are indeed a rich source of images, and one looks forward to continued analysis.

FIGURE R.7 Picture stone from Stora Hammars in Lärbro on Gotland, conventionally dated to the ninth or tenth century. The stone is c. 3 meters tall. Photo: Anders Andrén.

Rune Stones

Rök

With some 750 characters, the rune stone from Rök in the Swedish province of Östergötland is the longest known inscription (figure R.8). The granite stone stands over two meters tall and is more

FIGURE R.8 The rune stone at Rök, Östergötland, Sweden (Ög 136, Samnordisk runtextatabas). Photo: Anders Andrén.

than a meter wide, with runes on all four sides as well as on the top. Scholarly consensus dates the inscription to the early ninth century.

Although runologists are fairly certain about the transcription of the runes on the stone, despite manifold difficulties, they are far from agreed on the interpretation. What seems clear is that Rök is a memorial stone and thus presumably associated with death ritual, erected as it was by one Varin in memory of his dead son Væmod, and that it has three sequences of questions and answers that make allusions to the world of myth and legend. Besides the verse presented in the Introduction that will scan in the old Germanic alliterative meter, probably referring to the ancient hero Þiðrekr (Theodoric), there is an apparent reference to Þórr, toward the end of the inscription according to the (a?) standard reading. There are nearly as many interpretations of what Þórr would be doing here as there are scholars who write or have written about the inscription, and from the perspective of Old Norse mythology all we can really say is that Þórr may have figured in this unique monument that fixed oral tradition on stone in a most challenging, puzzling, and possibly riddling way: most of the inscription uses the standard runes of the period, but part uses an older version and various parts use a cipher.

Viking Age Inscriptions

The vast majority of rune stones are from the later Viking Age. Although they found throughout Scandinavia, the vast majority stand in the provinces of Uppland and Södermanland in the Mälar valley in central Sweden. Nearly all are memorials to a dead person from one of the surviving relatives or some other person with an attachment to the deceased. Overt references to Old Norse mythology are very rare, but there are a few. Perhaps the most interesting are the four inscriptions that call on Þórr to hallow the runes (figure R.9).

In the mythology the god most associated with runes is Óðinn, who credits himself with "taking them up" during his self-sacrifice on the world tree (*Hávamál* st. 138–45, at st. 139); earlier in the same poem (st. 80), the runes are said to be "of divine origin/which the great gods made/and the mighty sage coloured." If we are to guess the identity of the mighty sage, we would think first of Óðinn and hardly at all of Þórr. A possible explanation of the call to Þórr to hallow the runes is that the the later Viking Age was the time when the pre-Christian religion of Scandinavia met Christianity, and the meeting was most often portrayed as an opposition between Þórr and Christ.

FIGURE R.9 Rune stone from Sønder Kirkeby on Falster, Denmark, dated to about 1000 (DR 220, Samnordisk runtextdatabas). Between the ship at the top of the image (or side; the original orientation of the stone is not known) and the memorial inscription, dedicated by a man to his brother, is an invocation to Þórr. Photo: Roberto Fortuna, Nationalmuseet, København.

A handful of rune stones from the same period show obvious Þórr's hammers carved into the center of the stones (figure R.10). These are no doubt to be understood in the same way, with the symbol of Þórr being used in place of the cross, which is found on a great many rune stones of the period. (Here it is worth mentioning that many of the memorial inscriptions end "God rest his soul.")

FIGURE R.10 Rune stone at Stenkvista in Södermanland, from about 1000 (Sö 111, Samnordisk runtextdatabas), with an image of a Þórr's hammer, hanging upside down as would a Þórr's hammer amulet. The inscription is a memorial to a man by his sons. Their father's name appears in the horizontal line above the text band and the words "their father" in the vertical line running up to the hammer. Photo: Bengt A. Lundberg, Riksantikvarieämbetet, Stockholm.

An example of the meeting of these symbols is the intriguing mold from Denmark for making both (figure R.11).

FIGURE R.11 Mold for crosses and Þórr's hammer from Trendgaarden, Overlade, in Himmerland, Denmark (Nationalmuseet no. C24451). Photo: Lennart Larsen, Nationalmuseet, København.

The fact that the artisan could make two crosses for each Þórr's hammer suggests that business was more brisk for the Christian symbol, as would agree with the distribution of Christian and pre-Christian references and symbols on Viking Age rune stones.

REFERENCES

Abram, Christopher. 2011. *Myths of the Pagan North: The Gods of the Norsemen.* London and New York: Continuum.

Abram, Christopher. 2019. *Evergreen Ash: Ecology and Catastrophe in Old Norse Myth and Literature.* Charlottesville: University of Virginia Press.

Acker, Paul, trans. 1997. "The Saga of the People of Floi (Flóamanna Saga)." In *The Complete Sagas of Icelanders,* edited by Viðar Hreinsson et al., vol. 3. Reykjavík: Leifur Eiríksson Publishing.

Afzelius, Arvid August, trans. 1818. *Sæmund den vises Edda: Sånger af Nordens äldsta skalder.* Stockholm: I Deleens och Granbergs tryckerier.

Andrén, Anders. 2014. *Tracing Old Norse Cosmology: The World Tree, Middle Earth, and the Sun in Archaeological Perspectives.* Vägar till Midgård, 16. Lund: Nordic Academic Press.

Andrén, Anders, Kristina Jennbert, and Catharine Raudvere, eds. 2006. *Old Norse Religion in Long-Term Perspectives: Origins, Changes and Interactions—An International Conference in Lund, Sweden June 3–7, 2004.* Vägar till Midagård, 8. Lund: Nordic Academic Press.

Arngrímur Jónsson. 1609. *Crymogæa sive rerum Islandarum.* Copenhagen.

Arnold, Martin. 2011. *Thor: Myth to Marvel.* London and New York: Continuum.

Assmann, Jan. 2006. *Religion and Cultural Memory: Ten Studies.* Stanford, CA: Stanford University Press.

Bek-Pedersen, Karen. 2011. *The Norns in Old Norse Mythology.* Edinburgh: Dunedin.

Bellah, Robert N. 2011. *Religion in Human Evolution: From the Paleolithic to the Axial Age.* Cambridge, MA, and London: The Belknap Press of Harvard University Press.

Brink, Stefan, ed., in collaboration with Neil Price. 2008. *The Viking World.*
Abington: Routledge.

Brink, Stefan, and Lisa Collinson, eds. 2017. *Theorizing Old Norse Myth.* Acta
Scandinavica, 7, Turnhout: Brepols.

Buisson, Ludwig. 1976. *Der Bildstein Ardre VIII auf Gotland: Göttermythen,
Heldensagen und Jenseitsglaube der Germanen im 8. Jahrhundert n. Chr.*
Abhandlungen der Akademie der Wissenschaften in Göttingen,
Philologisch-Historische Klasse, Dritte Folge, 102. Göttingen:
Vandenhoeck & Ruprecht.

Byatt, A. S. 2011. *Ragnarök: The End of the Gods.* Edinburgh etc.: Canongate.

Clunies Ross, Margaret. 1994. *Prolonged Echoes: Old Norse Myth in Medieval
Northern Society.* Vol. 1: *The Myths.* Viking Collection, 7. [Odense:]
Odense University Press.

Clunies Ross, Margaret. 1998. *Prolonged Echoes: Old Norse Myth in Medieval
Northern Society.* Vol. 2: *The Reception of Norse Myth in Medieval Iceland.*
Viking Collection, 10. [Odense:] Odense University Press.

Clunies Ross, Margaret, ed. 2000. *Old Norse Literature and Society.*
Cambridge Studies in Medieval Literature, 43. Cambridge: Cambridge
University Press.

Clunies Ross, Margaret, ed. 2003. *Old Norse Myths, Literature and Society.* The
Viking Collection, 14. [Odense:] University Press of Southern Denmark.

Clunies Ross, Margaret, ed. 2017a. "Bragi inn gamli Boddason, Þórr's Fishing."
In *Skaldic Poetry of the Scandinavian Middle Ages.* Vol. 3,1: *Poetry from
Treatises on Poetics, Part 1,* edited by Kari Ellen Gade in collaboration
with Edith Marold, 46–53. Turnhout: Brepols.

Clunies Ross, Margaret, ed. 2017b. "Eysteinn Valdason, Poem about Þórr."
In *Skaldic Poetry of the Scandinavian Middle Ages.* Vol. 3,1: *Poetry from
Treatises on Poetics, Part 1,* edited by Kari Ellen Gade in collaboration
with Edith Marold, 185–88. Turnhout: Brepols.

Clunies Ross, Margaret, ed. 2017c. "Gamli gnævaðarskáld, Poem about Þórr."
In *Skaldic Poetry of the Scandinavian Middle Ages.* Vol. 3,1: *Poetry from
Treatises on Poetics, Part 1,* edited by Kari Ellen Gade in collaboration
with Edith Marold, 189–90. Turnhout: Brepols.

Clunies Ross, Margaret, ed. 2017d. "Þjóðólfr ór Hvíni, Haustlǫng." In *Skaldic
Poetry of the Scandinavian Middle Ages.* Vol. 3,1: *Poetry from Treatises on
Poetics, Part 1,* edited by Kari Ellen Gade in collaboration with Edith
Marold, 431–63. Turnhout: Brepols.

Clunies Ross, Margaret, ed. 2017e. "Þorbjǫrn dísarskáld, Poem about Þórr."
In *Skaldic Poetry of the Scandinavian Middle Ages.* Vol. 3,1: *Poetry from*

Treatises on Poetics, Part 1, edited by Kari Ellen Gade in collaboration with Edith Marold, 470–72. Turnhout: Brepols.

Clunies Ross, Margaret, ed. 2017f. "Qlvir hnúfa, Poem about Þórr." In *Skaldic Poetry of the Scandinavian Middle Ages*. Vol. 3,1: *Poetry from Treatises on Poetics, Part 1*, edited by Kari Ellen Gade in collaboration with Edith Marold, 491. Turnhout: Brepols.

Clunies Ross, Margaret, ed. 2018a. *The Pre-Christian Religions of the North: Research and Reception*, vol. 1: *From the Middle Ages to c. 1830*. Turnhout: Brepols.

Clunies Ross, Margaret, ed. 2018b. *The Pre-Christian Religions of the North: Research and Reception*, vol. 2: *From c. 1830 to the Present*. Turnhout: Brepols.

Clunies Ross, Margaret, and Lars Lönnroth. 1999. "The Norse Muse: Report from an International Research Project." *Alvisssmál* 9: 3–28.

Cnattingius, Anders Jacob, trans. 1819. *Snorre Sturlesons Edda: Samt Skalda: Öfversättning från skandinaviska forn-språket*. Stockholm: Elméns och Granbergs tryckeri.

Crawford, Jackson, trans. 2015. *The Poetic Edda: Stories of the Norse Gods and Heroes*. Indianapolis and Cambridge: Hacket Publishing Company.

Dodds, Jeramy, trans. 2011. *The Poetic Edda*. Toronto: Coach House Press.

Dronke, Ursula, ed. and trans. 1997. *The Poetic Edda*. Vol. 2: *Mythological Poems*. Oxford: Clarendon.

Dronke, Ursula, ed. and trans. 2011. *The Poetic Edda*. Vol. 3: *Mythological Poems*. Oxford: Clarendon.

DuBois, Thomas A. 1999. *Nordic Religions in the Viking Age*. Philadelphia: University of Pennsylvania Press.

Dumézil, Georges. 1973. *Gods of the Ancient Northmen*. Ed. Einar Haugen, trans. John Lindow et al. Berkeley and Los Angeles: University of California Press.

Dumézil, Georges. 1987. *From Myth to Fiction: The Saga of Hadingus*. Trans. Derek Coltman. Chicago: University of Chicago Press.

Edda Sæmundar hinns Fróda. Edda rhythmica seu antiqvior, vulgo Sæmundina dicta . . . Ex codice Bibliothecæ regiæ hafniensis pergameno. Vol. I: *Odas mythologicas, non Resenio edita. . . .* 1778. Vol. III: *Poeseos vetustissimae Scandinavorum trifolium . . .* 1828. Copenhagen: Argnamagnæan Commission and Gyldendal.

Ekrem, Inger, and Lars Boje Mortensen, eds., and Peter Fisher, trans. 2003. *Historia Norwegie*. [Copenhagen:] Museum Tusculanum Press.

Faulkes, Anthony, trans. 1987. *Snorri Sturluson: Edda*. Everyman. London: J. M. Dent.

Frank, Roberta. 1978. *Old Norse Court Poetry: The Dróttkvætt Stanza*. Islandica, 42. Ithaca, NY, and London: Cornell University Press.

von Friesen, C. 1883. "Götiska förbundet." *Nordisk familiebok* 6: 426–30. Stockholm: Expeditionen af Nordisk familjebok/Gernandts boktryckeriaktiebolag. http://runeberg.org/nfaf/0219.html. Last accessed December 13, 2017.

Friis-Jensen, Karsten, ed., and Peter Fisher, trans. 2015. *Saxo Grammaticus: Gesta Danorum—The History of the Danes*. Oxford Medieval Texts. Oxford: Clarendon.

Fulk, R. D., ed. 2012a. "Eiríksmál." In *Skaldic Poetry of the Scandinavian Middle Ages, I: Poetry from the Kings Sagas*, edited by Diana Whaley, Part 2, 1003–13. Turnhout: Brepols.

Fulk, R. D., ed. 2012b. "Eyvindr skáldaspillir Finnsson." In *Skaldic Poetry of the Scandinavian Middle Ages, I: Poetry from the Kings Sagas*, edited by Diana Whaley, Part 1, 171–94. Turnhout: Brepols.

Fulk, R. D., ed. 2017. "Vetrliði Sumarliðason." In *Skaldic Poetry of the Scandinavian Middle Ages*. Vol. 3,1: *Poetry from Treatises on Poetics, Part 1*, edited by Kari Ellen Gade in collaboration with Edith Marold, 425–26. Turnhout: Brepols.

Gaiman, Neil. 2001. *American Gods*. New York: William Morrow.

Gaiman, Neil. 2017. *Norse Mythology*. New York: W. W. Norton.

García Losqueño, Irene, Olof Sundqvist, and Declan Taggart, eds. 2020. *Making the Profane Sacred in the Viking Age: Essays in Honour of Stefan Brink*. Medieval Texts and Cultures of Northern Europe, 32. Turnhout: Brepols.

Gjessing, G. A., trans. 1866. *Den ædre Edda: Norrøna oldkvad*. Kristianssand: S. A. Steen.

Göransson, Johan, ed. and trans. 1746. *De Yfverborna Atlingars, eller, Sviogötars ok Nordmänners, Edda . . .: Hyperboreorum Atlantiorum, seu, Suigotorum et Nordmannorum Edda . . .: iam demum versione Svionica donata, accedente Latina; una cum praefatione de Eddae antiquitate indole . . . .* Uppsala: Hecht.

Göransson, Johan, ed. and trans. 1750. *De yfverborna atlingers eller Sviogöthars ok Nordmänners patriarkaliska lära, eller sådan hon var före Odhin II:s tid; Af Sämund hin frode på Island efter gamla runoböcker år Chr. 1090 afskrefven; men nu efter trenne Kongl. Antiquite: Archivet tilhöriga gsöthiska handskrifter med svensk öfversättning*. Stockholm: Jakob Merkell.

Gosse, Edmund. 1911. "Öhlenschläger, Adam Gottlob." In *Encyclopædia Britannica* vol. 20. https://en.wikisource.org/wiki/1911_Encyclopædia_Britannica/Öhlenschläger,_Adam_Gottlob. Last accessed December 13, 2017.

Granlund, John. 1976 (1951). "Kommentar." In *Historia om de nordiska folken…*, Vol. 1, 265–405. Stockholm: Gidlund.

Grimm, Jacob. *Deutsche Mythologie*. Göttingen: Dieterichsche Buchhandlung.

Grimm, Jacob, and Wilhelm Grimm. 1812–1815. *Kinder- und Hausmärchen*. Berlin: Verl. der Realschulbuchh.

Grimm, Jacob, and Wilhelm Grimm, trans. 1815. *Die Lieder der alten Edda*. Berlin: Verl. der Realschulbuchh.

Grundtvig, N. F. S. 1808. *Nordens mythologie eller udsigt over Eddalæren for dannede mænd, der ei selv ere mytologer*. Copenhagen: J. H. Schubothes Boghandling.

Grundtvig, N. F. S. 1832. *Nordens mythologie eller Sindbilled-Sprog historisk-poetisk udviklet og oplyst*. Copenhagen: J. H. Schubothes Boghandling.

Gunnel, Terry, and Annette Lassen, eds. 2013. *The Nordic Apocalypse: Approaches to Vǫluspá and Nordic Days of Judgment*. Acta Scandinavica, 2. Turnhout: Brepols.

Hafner, Tina. 2008. *Peter Madsens Valhalla: Studien zur Rezeption altwestnordischer Mythen im modernen Comic*. Munich: Grin Verlag.

Haraldur Bernharðsson. 2007. "Old Icelandic Ragnarök and Ragnarökkr." In Verba Docenti: Studies in Historical and Indo-European Linguistics Presented to Jay H. Jasanoff, edited by Alan J. Nussbaum, 25–38. Ann Arbor: Beach Stave Press.

Harris, Joseph. 2017. "Traditions of Eddic Scholarship." In *A Handbook to Eddic Poetry: Myths and Legends of Early Scandinavia*, edited by Carolyne Larrington, Judy Quinn, and Brittany Schorn, 33–57. Cambridge: Cambridge University Press.

Hastrup, Kirsten. 1985. *Culture and History in Medieval Iceland: An Anthropological Analysis of Structure and Change*. Oxford: Clarendon.

Hauck, Karl. 1992. "Der religions- und sozialgeschichtliche Quellenwert der völkerwanderungszeitlichen Goldbrakteaten." In *Germanische Religionsgeschichte: Quellen und Quellenprobleme*, edited by Heinrich Beck, Detlev Ellmers, and Kurt Schier, 229–69. Ergänzungsbände zum Reallexikon der germanischen Altertumskunde, 5. Berlin and New York: de Gruyter.

Heimir Pálsson, ed., and Anthony Faulkes, trans. 2012. *Snorri Sturluson: The Uppsala Edda: DG 11 4to*. [London:] Viking Society for Northern Research/University College London.

Helgason, Jón Karl. *See* Jón Karl Helgason.

Helle, Knut, ed. 2003. *The Cambridge History of Scandinavia*, vol. 1: *Prehistory to 1520*. Cambridge: Cambridge University Press.

Herder, Johannes Gottfried. 1778–1779. *Volkslieder: Nebst untermischten andern Stücken.* 2 vols. Leipzig: Weygand.

Hermann, Pernille, Stephen A. Mitchell, and Jens Peter Schjødt, eds., with Amber J. Rose. 2017. *Old Norse Mythology: Comparative Perspectives.* Cambridge, MA, and London: Harvard University Press for the Milman Parry Collection.

Hollander, Lee M., trans. 1964. *Heimskringla: History of the Kings of Norway—By Snorri Sturluson.* Austin: American Scandinavian Foundation/The University of Texas Press.

Jón Karl Helgason. 2017. *Echoes of Valhalla: The Afterlife of the Eddas and Sagas.* London: Reaktion.

Jónsson, Arngrímur. See Arngrímur Jónsson.

Kaplan, Marrill, and Timothy R. Tangherlini, eds. 2012. *News from Other Worlds: Studies in Nordic Folklore, Mythology and Culture: In Honor of John F. Lindow.* Wildcat Canyon Advanced Seminars, Occasional Monographs, 1. Berkeley and Los Angeles, CA: North Pinehurst Press.

King, David. 2005. *Finding Atlantis: A True Story of Genius, Madness, and an Extraordinary Quest for a Lost World.* New York: Harmony Books.

Kopár, Lilla. 2016. "Eddic Poetry and the Imagery of Stone Monuments." In *A Handbook to Eddic Poetry: Myths and Legends of Early Scandinavia*, ed. Carolyne Larrington, Judy Quinn, and Brittany Schorn, 136–44. Cambridge: Cambridge University Press.

Kure, Henning. 2010. *I begyndelsen var skriget: Vikingetidens myter om skabelsen.* [Copenhagen:] Gyldendal.

Larrington, Carolyne, trans. 2014. *The Poetic Edda.* Rev. ed. Oxford World's Classics. Oxford etc.: Oxford University Press.

Larrington, Carolyne. 2017. *The Norse Myths: A Guide to the Gods and Heroes.* London : Thames & Hudson.

Larrington, Carolyne, Judy Quinn, and Brittany Schorn, eds. 2016. *A Handbook to Eddic Poetry: Myths and Legends of Early Scandinavia.* Cambridge: Cambridge University Press, 2016.

Lincoln, Bruce. 1999. *Theorizing Myth: Narrative, Ideology, and Scholarship.* Chicago and London: The University of Chicago Press.

Lindow, John. 1988. *Scandinavian Mythology: An Annotated Bibliography.* Garland Folklore Bibliographies, 13; Garland Reference Library of the Humanities, 393. New York and London: Garland Publishing.

Lindow, John. 1997. *Murder and Vengeance among the Gods: Baldr in Scandinavian Mythology.* FF Communications, 262. Helsinki: Suomalainen Tiedeakatemia/Academia Scientiarum Fennica.

Lindow, John. 2001. *Norse Mythology: A Guide to the Gods, Heroes, Rituals, and Beliefs*. Oxford etc.: Oxford University Press.

Lindow, John. 2014. "Mythic Narrative Modes as Exemplified in the Story of Þórr's Journey to Geirrøðr (and His Daughters)." In *Nordic Mythologies: Interpretations, Intersections and Institutions*, edited by Timothy R. Tangherlini, 3–18. Wildcat Canyon Seminars: Mythology, 1. Berkeley and Los Angeles: North Pinehurst Press.

Lindow, John, and Jens Peter Schjødt. 2020. "The Divine, the Human, and In Between." In *The Pre-Christian Religions of the North: History and Structures*, edited by Jens Peter Schjødt, John Lindow, and Anders Andrén, vol. 2: 951–87. Turnhout: Brepols.

Lindqvist, Sune. 1941–42. Gotlands Bildsteine, 2 vols. Stockholm: Wahlström & Widstrand.

Ling, Pehr Henrik. 1819. *Eddornas sinnebildslära, för olärde framställd*. Stockholm: Cederborgska boktryckeriet.

Lorenz, Gottfried. 1984. *Gylfaginning: Texte, Übersetzung, Kommentar*. Texte zur Forschung, 48. Darmstadt: Wissenschaftliche Buchgesellschaft.

Madsen, Peter (art), Henning Kure (script), et al. 1991. *Ormen i dybet*, Valhalla 7. Copenhagen: Forlaget Carlsen.

Magnus, Olaus. 1555. *Historia de Gentibus Septentrionalibus. . . .* Rome.

Mallet, Paul Henri. 1755. *Introduction à L'histoire de Dannemarc ou l'on traite de la religion, des mœurs, des lois, et des usages des anciens Danois*. Geneva: Barde Manget/Paris: Buisson.

Mallet, Paul Henri. 1756. *Introduction à L'histoire de Dannemarc*. Vol. 2: *Monumens de la mythologie et de la poésie des Celtes et particulierement des anciens Scandinaves*. Geneva: Barde Manget.

Marold, Edith. 1998. "Die Augen des Herrschers." In *Beretning fra syttende tværfaglige vikingesymposium*, edited by Dietrich Meier, 7–29. Aarhus: Hikiun/Afdeling for Middelalder-arkæologi, Aarhus Universitet.

Marold, Edith, et al., eds. 2017. "Úlfr Uggason, Húsdrápa." In *Skaldic Poetry of the Scandinavian Middle Ages*. Vol. 3,1: *Poetry from Treatises on Poetics, Part 1*, edited by Kari Ellen Gade in collaboration with Edith Marold, 402–24. Turnhout: Brepols.

McKinnell, John. 2005. *Meeting the Other in Norse Myth and Legend*. Cambridge: D. S. Brewer.

McKinnell, John. 2014. *Essays on Eddic Poetry*. Ed. Donata Kick and John D. Shafer. Toronto, Buffalo, and London: University of Toronto Press.

McTurk, Rory, ed. 2005. *A Companion to Old-Norse Icelandic Literature and Culture*. Oxford: Blackwell.

Meulengracht Sørensen, Preben. 1983. *The Unmanly Man: Concepts of Sexual Defamation in Early Northern Society*. Trans. Joan Turville-Petre. Viking Series, 1. [Odense:] Odense University Press.

Meulengracht Sørensen, Preben 1986. "Thor's Fishing Expedition." In *Words and Objects: Towards a Dialogue between Archaeology and History of Religion*, edited by Gro Steinsland: 257–78. Oslo: Universitetsforlaget. Reprint in *The Poetic Edda: Essays on Old Norse Mythology*, edited by Paul Acker and Carolyne Larrington: 119–37. London and New York: Routledge.

Meyer, Niels I., K. Helveg Petersen, and Villy Sørensen. 1978. *Oprør fra midten*. Copenhagen: Gyldendal. English translation: *Revolt from the Center*. London and Boston: M. Boyars, 1981.

Mitchell, Stephen A. 2011. *Witchcraft and Magic in the Nordic Middle Ages*. Philadelphia and Oxford: University of Pennsylvania Press.

Mitchell, Stephen A. 2020. "Magic and Religion." In *The Pre-Christian Religions of the North: History and Structures*, edited by Jens Peter Schjødt, John Lindow, and Anders Andrén, vol. 2: 644–70. Turnhout: Brepols.

Møinichen, Jacob Bærent. 1801. *Nordiske folks overtroe, guder, fabler og helte: Indtil Frode 7 tider—I bogstavordning*. Copenhagen: P. M. Liunge.

Nyerup, Rasmus, trans. 1808. *Edda eller hedenske skandinavernes gudelære*. Copenhagen: Andreas Sedelins forlag.

O'Donoghue, Heather. 2007. *From Asgard to Valhalla: The Remarkable History of the Norse Myths*. London and New York: I. B. Taurus.

O'Donoghue, Heather. 2014. *English Poetry and Old Norse Myth: A History*. Oxford University Press.

Oehlenschläger, Adam. 1819. *Nordens guder: Et episk digt*. Copenhagen: H. F. Popp.

Oehrl, Sigmund 2006. *Zur Deutung anthropomorpher und theriomorpher Bilddarstellungen auf den spätwikingerzeitlichen Runensteinen Schwedens*. Wiener Studien zur Skandinavistik, 16. Vienna: Praesens.

Oosten, Jarich G. 1985. *The War of the Gods: The Social Code in Indo-European Mythology*. London etc.: Routledge and Kegan Paul.

Orchard, Andy. 1997. *Dictionary of Norse Myth and Legend*. London: Cassell.

Orchard, Andy, trans. 2011. *The Elder Edda: A Book of Viking Lore*. London etc.: Penguin.

Pálsson, Heimir. *See* Heimir Pálsson.

Percy, Thomas, trans. 1770. *Northern Antiquities, or, an Historical Account of the Manners, Customs, Religion and Laws, Maritime Expeditions and Discoveries, Language and Literature of the Ancient Scandinavians*. 2 vols. London: T. Carnan.

Perkins, Richard. 2001. *Thor the Wind-Raiser and the Eyrarland Image.* Viking Society for Northern Research Text Series, 15. London: Viking Society for Northern Research/University College London.

Pesch, Alexandra. 2007. *Die Goldbrakteaten der Völkerwanderungszeit: Thema und Variation.* Ergänzungsbände zum Reallexikon der germanischen Altertumskunde, 36. Berlin and New York: de Gruyter.

Petersen, William, trans. 1914. *The Dialogues of Publius Cornelius Tacitus.* Loeb Classical Library. Cambridge, MA: Harvard University Press/ London: William Heineman.

Poole, Russell, ed. 2012. "Eyvindr skáldaspillir Finnson: Háleygjatal." In *Skaldic Poetry of the Scandinavian Middle Ages, I: Poetry from the Kings Sagas,* edited by Diana Whaley, Part 1, 195–213. Turnhout: Brepols.

Price, Neil. 2019. *The Viking Way: Magic and Mind in Late Iron Age Scandinavia.* Oxford and Phildadelphia: Oxbow Books.

Pulsiano, Philipp, and Kirsten Wolf, eds. 1993. *Medieval Scandinavia: An Encyclopedia.* New York and London: Garland Publishing.

Quinn, Judy, Kate Heslop, and Tarrin Wills, eds. 2007. *Learning and Understanding in the Old Norse World: Essays in Honour of Margaret Clunies Ross.* Medieval Texts and Cultures of Northern Europe, 18. Turnhout: Brepols.

Raudvere, Catharina, and Jens Peter Schjødt, eds. 2012. *More Than Mythology: Narratives, Ritual Practices and Regional Distribution in Pre-Christian Scandinavian Religion.* Lund: Nordic Academic Press.

Rudbeck, Olof. 1679–1702. *Atland, eller Manheim: Atlantica sive Manheim. . . .* Uppsala.

Rühs, Friedrich. 1812. *Die Edda: Nebst einer Einleitung über nordische Poesie und Mythologie. . . .* Berlin: Realschulebuchhandlung.

Rühs, Friedrich. 1815. *Über die Ansprüche der Juden auf das deutsche Bürgerrecht.* Berlin: Realschulebuchhandlung.

Schjødt, Jens Peter. 2008. *Initiation between Two Worlds: Structure and Symbolism in Pre-Christian Scandinavian Religion.* The Viking Collection, 17. [Odense:] The University Press of Southern Denmark.

Schjødt, Jens Peter. 2020. "Kings and Rulers." In *The Pre-Christian Religions of the North: History and Structures,* edited by Jens Peter Schjødt, John Lindow, and Anders Andrén, vol. 2: 529–57. Turnhout: Brepols.

Schjødt, Jens Peter, John Lindow, and Anders Andrén, eds. 2020. *Pre-Christian Religions of the North: History and Structures.* 4 vols. Turnhout: Brepols.

von Schnurbein, Stephanie. 1992. *Religion als Kulturkritik: Neugermanisches Heidentum im 20. Jahrhundert.* Heidelberg: Winter.

von Schnurbein, Stephanie. 1993. *Göttertrost in Wednezeiten: Neugermanisches Heidentum zwischen New Age und Rechtsradikalismus.* Munich: Claudius-Verlag.

von Schnurbein, Stephanie. 2016. *Norse Revival: Transformations of Germanic Neo-Paganism.* Leiden: Brill.

von Schnurbein, Stephanie. 2018. "Germanic Neo-Paganism." In *The Pre-Christian Religions of the North: Research and Reception*, vol. 2: *From c. 1830 to the Present.*, edited by Margaret Clunies Ross, 371–97. Turnhout: Brepols.

Schröder, Franz Rolf. 1955. "Das Hymirlied: Zur Frage verblasster Mythen in den Götterliedern der Edda." *Arkiv för nordisk filologi* 70: 1–40.

Schulz, Katja. 2004. *Riesen: Von Wissenhütern und Wildnisbewohnern in Edda und Saga.* Heidelberg: Winter.

Simek, Rudolf. 1993. *Dictionary of Northern Mythology.* Trans. Angela Hall. Cambridge: D. S. Brewer.

Sørensen, Villy. 1988. *Ragnarok: En gudefortælling.* [Copenhagen:] Dansklærerforening [/ Gyldendal]. English translation: *The Downfall of the Gods: Ragnarok.* Trans. Paula Hostrup-Jensen. Lincoln: University of Nebraska Press, 1989.

Sundqvist, Olof. 2002. *Freyr's Offspring: Rulers and Religion in Ancient Svea Society.* Historia Religionum, 21. Uppsala: Uppsala Universitet.

von Sydow, C. W. 1915. "Jätten Hymes bägere." *Danske studier* 1915: 113–50.

Taggart, Declan. 2018. *How Thor Lost His Thunder: The Changing Faces of an Old Norse God.* Routledge Research in Medieval Studies, 14. London: Routledge.

Tangherlini, Timothy R., ed. 2014. *Nordic Mythologies: Interpretations, Intersections, and Institutions.* The Wildcat Canyon Advanced Seminars: Mythology, 1. Berkeley and Los Angeles, CA: North Pinehurst Press.

Tolley, Clive. 2009. *Shamanism in Norse Myth and Magic.* 2 vols. FF Communications, 296–97. Helsinki: Suomalainen Tiedeakatemia/ Academia Scientiarum Fennica.

Turville-Petre, Gabriel. 1964. *Myth and Religion of the North: The Religion of Ancient Scandinavia.* New York: Holt, Rinehart, & Winston.

Vikstrand, Per. 2006. "Ásgarðr, Miðgarðr, and Útgarðr: A Linguistic Approach to a Classical Problem." In *Old Norse Religion in Long-Term Perspectives: Origins, Changes, and Interaction: An International Conference in Lund, Sweden, June 3–7, 2004*, ed. Anders Andrén, Kristina Jennbert, and Catharina Raudvere, 354–57. Vägar till Midgård, 4. Lund: Nordic Academic Press.

de Vries, Jan. 1955–1956. *Altgermanische Religionsgeschichte*, 3rd ed. 2 vols. Grundriss der germanischen Philologie 12:1–2. Berlin: W. de Gruyter.

de Vries, Jan. 1961. *Altnordisches etymologisches Wörterbuch*. Leiden: Brill.

Wägner, Wilhelm. 1880. *Asgard and the Gods: Tales and Traditions of Our Northern Ancestors Told for Boys and Girls*. Adapted by M. W. McDowell and edited by W. S. W. Anson. London: W. Swan Sonnenschein & Allen.

Wanner, Kevin J. 2008. *Snorri Sturluson and the Edda: The Conversion of Cultural Capital in Medieval Scandinavia*. Toronto, Buffalo, and London: University of Toronto Press.

Wawn, Andrew. 2000. *The Vikings and the Victorians: Inventing the Old North in Nineteenth-Century Britain*. Cambridge: D. S. Brewer.

West, M. L. 2007. *Indo-European Poetry and Myth*. Oxford etc.: Oxford University Press.

Wicker, Nancy, and Henrik Williams. 2012. "Bracteates and Runes: Review Article." *Futhark—International Journal of Runic Studies* 3: 151–213.

Wikström af Edholm, Klas, et al., eds. *Myth, Materiality, and Lived Religion: In Merovingian and Viking Scandinavia*. Stockholm Studies in Comparative Religion, 40. Stockholm: Stockholm University Press.

Wolf, Alois. 1977. "Sehweisen und Darstellungsfragen in der Gylfaginning: Thors Fischfang." *Skandinavistik* 7: 1–27.

Zernack, Julia. 2018. "A Key Work for the Reception History of Norse Mythology and Poetry: Paul Henri Mallet's *History of the Danish Empire* and its European Impact." In *The Pre-Christian Religions of the North: Research and Reception*, vol. 1: *From the Middle Ages to c. 1839*, edited by Margaret Clunies Ross, 281–313. Turnhout: Brepols.

INDEX

Figures are indicated by *f* following the page number

Note: diacritics are ignored for alphabetization, and þ follows z at the end of the alphabet